CANADA

Minnesota

Lake Superior

Lake Itasca

Maine

Vermont

New Hampshire

Mt. Marcy
Lake Tear of the Clouds
Adirondack Mountains

New

Minneapolis

Wisconsin

Lake Huron

Lake Michigan

Michigan

Lake Ontario

Mohawk River Albany

Hudson RIVER

Massachusetts

Erie Canal

New York

Rhode Island

Sioux City

Iowa

Moline

Lake Erie

Allegheny River

Pennsylvania

Connecticut

New York City

New Jersey

Delaware

maha

St. Joseph

Illinois

Indiana

Ohio

Great Serpent Mound

Pittsburgh

Wheeling

Monongahela River

Grave Creek

Maryland

Hannibal

Cincinnati

West Virginia

Kansas City

Independence

St. Charles

St. Louis

Cahokia

Ohio Valley

Louisville

Ohio RIVER

Virginia

Appalachian Mountains

Missouri

Kentucky

oma

Cairo

New Madrid

Mississippi River

Tennessee

North Carolina

Arkansas

Memphis

South Carolina

Atlantic Ocean

Mississippi

Alabama

Georgia

Vicksburg

Louisiana

New Orleans

Florida

Gulf of Mexico

River
Roads
West America's First Highways

PETER AND CONNIE ROOP

CALKINS CREEK
Honesdale, Pennsylvania

To Bill, who brought us together and inspired our love of history

Acknowledgments

The authors would like to thank the following for their help in researching this book: the National Mississippi River Museum and Aquarium; Rivers Odyssey West; the Delta Queen Steamboat Company; and the staffs of the Mesa Verde National Park, Grand Canyon National Park, the John Wesley Powell Memorial Museum, the Mud Island River Park, Jefferson National Expansion Memorial, Lewis & Clark State Historic Site, Fort Clatsop, Fort Mandan, Rocky Mountain National Park, and the Oregon Historical Society.

We would also like to thank Peter C. Mancall, director of the USC–Huntington Early Modern Studies Institute and professor of history and anthropology, University of Southern California, for reading the manuscript. Special thanks to our editor and friend Carolyn P. Yoder, who kept us "paddling" even when waves, rapids, and storms seemed as if they would swamp our boat.

CALKINS CREEK
An Imprint of Boyds Mills Press, Inc.
815 Church Street
Honesdale, Pennsylvania 18431

FRONT JACKET: Published about 1856, this print by Currier and Ives shows a bird's-eye view of New York City with Battery Park in the foreground and a busy Hudson River on the left and the East River on the right.
BACK JACKET: The Colorado River

Contents

THE HUDSON

THE OHIO

THE MISSISSIPPI

THE MISSOURI

THE RIO GRANDE

THE COLORADO

THE COLUMBIA

Mississippi River

Should you ask me, whence these stories?

Whence these legends and traditions,

With the odours of the forest,

With the dew and damp of meadows,

With the curling smoke of wigwams,

With the rushing of great rivers,

With their frequent repetitions,

And their wild reverberations,

As of thunder in the mountains?

—"The Song of Hiawatha"
   Henry Wadsworth Longfellow,
   American poet (1807–1882)

Introduction

The Hudson. The Ohio. The Mississippi. The Missouri. The Rio Grande. The Colorado. The Columbia. These rivers, America's first highways, echo through our history.

Long before pioneer axes cut trails through the wilderness, rivers were the roads people traveled. Curving between forests, carving out canyons, slicing through prairies, and splashing down mountains, rivers were the first roads into the American wilderness.

Each rippling, rushing river has its own unique voice telling thrilling tales about our expanding nation. The people who lived by, explored, and traveled on the rivers added their distinct expressions through stories, songs, journals, and sayings. Together, the rivers and their people created a powerful current running through our past.

The first travelers on America's river roads were Indians hunting, fishing, and trading. In the 1500s and 1600s the songs of strong voyageurs echoed along these same shores. In the 1700s hardy traders bartered along winding riverbanks. In 1804 the Lewis and Clark expedition paddled, pulled, poled, and sailed more than two thousand miles up the twisting Missouri River. They crossed the Rocky Mountains to race down the rapid Columbia to the Pacific Ocean. Their heroic efforts earned them the honor of becoming the first citizens of the United States to cross the continent.

Throughout the 1800s settlers, like ax-swinging Abraham Lincoln, rode rough log rafts searching for a place to call home. Joining the settlers round the river bends puffed hundreds, then thousands of hissing steamboats. River pilot Samuel Clemens, born and raised along the Mississippi, became the author we know as Mark Twain. Through his words, Tom Sawyer, Huckleberry Finn, and Jim shared their river adventures with the world.

In the mid-1800s thousands of stouthearted pioneers rolled west in their covered wagons along the Oregon, California, or Sante Fe trails. For most, their overland journeys began on the Missouri River. In 1849 people eager for gold rushed west to strike it rich.

Through the 1800s and early 1900s, millions of immigrants followed the Hudson River to the Erie Canal, then sailed the Great Lakes seeking a better life. Thousands poured down the Ohio or onto the mighty Mississippi, all moving west, all searching for new homes.

Through our history, from the Atlantic to the Pacific, from the past to the present, rivers have been America's roads west. This book is about how America's major river roads—the Hudson (and Erie Canal), the Ohio, the Mississippi, the Missouri, the Colorado, the Rio Grande, and the Columbia—each contributed its own unique story to our history.

And from among those hills a mighty, deep-mouthed

river ran into the sea.

—European explorer Giovanni Verrazano,
   captain of the French ship *Dauphin*, 1524

I've got a mule, her name is Sal,

Fifteen miles on the Erie Canal.

She's a good ol' worker and a good ol' pal,

Fifteen miles on the Erie Canal.

We've hauled some barges in our day,

Filled with lumber, coal, and hay,

And we know every inch of the way,

From Albany to Buffalo.

—Traditional American folk song
   about traveling on the Erie Canal

The Hudson River and the Erie Canal

The Headwaters of the Hudson

A stream spills out of mile-high Summit Water in New York's Adirondack Mountains. Tumbling down the steep slopes, this narrow stream eventually becomes the Hudson River. Slightly more than three hundred miles later, the Hudson flows past Manhattan's man-made towers, bathes the Statue of Liberty's copper feet, and pours its waters into the Atlantic Ocean.

Twelve thousand years ago, mile-thick glaciers shaped the Adirondack Mountains. The glaciers gouged the bedrock, bulldozed the earth, and carved deep valleys. Hundreds of ponds and lakes were left behind when the glaciers melted. One pond, glittering Summit Water, became the Hudson's source. Summit Water shimmers on Mount Marcy, the Adirondack's tallest peak. The Indians called this towering mountain *Tahawus,* "Cloudsplitter." In 1872 the naturalist and explorer Verplanck Colvin became the first white American to see the river's humble headwaters trickling out of Summit Water. Colvin described Summit Water as an "unpretending tear of the clouds." Summit Water became Lake Tear of the Clouds.

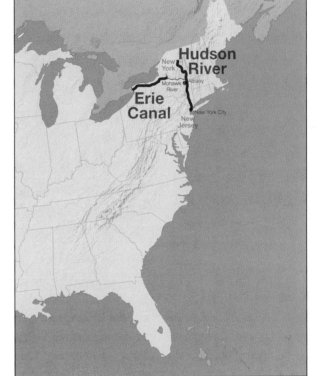

The Indian World

Ten thousand years before Colvin climbed Cloudsplitter, Indians had settled in the region. The Raritans, Hackensacks, Tappans, Haverstraws, Catskills, Manhattans, Mohicans, and Wappingers claimed the region as their home. They called the Hudson *Muhheakunnuk,* "The Water That Flows Two Ways." Twice a day, salty water from the Atlantic Ocean rides the tide up the Hudson Valley. Freshwater streaming downstream meets this ocean water, creating a river that flows "two ways."

In the forests of the region, the Indians built wigwams and longhouses from the wood and bark of the plentiful maple, oak, hickory, and birch trees. Men and

boys hunted deer, bear, wolf, moose, ducks, and geese. They caught shad, sturgeon, herring, and bass in the Muhheakunnuk.

Women and girls planted and harvested the Three Sisters: the corn, beans, and squash that flourished in the rich soil. They tanned animal skins to make shirts, skirts, moccasins, and breechclouts, decorating them with dyed porcupine quills. They cooked meals and dried meat to eat during the long, cold winters.

At night around their fires, the Indians told tales of *Minewawa,* the goddess of the Muhheakunnuk Valley, who hurled lightning and hung the moon in the sky. They told stories about *Jeebi,* the ghost who wailed like a whip-poorwill, and about the tiny *Pukwidjinnies* and about the mighty *Windigos,* who fought tremendous battles using whole oak trees as clubs.

The Arrival of the European Explorers

Indian life in the Hudson Valley changed with the coming of the Europeans in 1524. That year Italian explorer Giovanni Verrazano became the first European to see the Hudson. Verrazano, captain of the *Dauphin,* was hired by King Francis I of France to explore the coast of North America. King Francis wanted to know if there was a waterway west across North America.

People who envisioned this water route across America to the Pacific Ocean called it the Northwest Passage. The European explorer who would discover the Northwest Passage would bring fame to himself and great wealth to his country.

THE NORTHWEST PASSAGE

For centuries, explorers unsuccessfully searched for the Northwest Passage, unaware that a waterway across America did not exist. The Dutch, the English, the French, and the Spanish were eager to be the first to find a fast way through North America to reach the riches of the Spice Islands of the East Indies. Their normal routes took a long, dangerous passage around Africa's southern tip. Even so, their cargoes of pepper, nutmeg, cinnamon, and other valuable spices sold for huge profits in Europe. After Columbus, European explorers hoped a waterway west through North America would be a priceless shortcut to the Pacific Ocean and the East Indies. The search for the Northwest Passage shaped the history of the continent for three hundred years.

With the *Dauphin* anchored at the mouth of the Hudson, Verrazano wrote: "We found a pleasant place below steep little hills. And from among those hills a mighty, deep-mouthed river ran into the sea." Verrazano explored what is now New York Harbor before continuing his journey up the coast. He never sailed up the Hudson.

The Hudson River begins high atop Mount Marcy in New York's Adirondack Mountains. It trickles out of Lake Tear of the Clouds as it begins its journey to the Atlantic Ocean.

Indians inhabited Manhattan Island for thousands of years. They often built their longhouses near the shore for easy access to food and water. A ship from Europe is anchored at the tip of Manhattan.

Henry Hudson was a determined explorer. One of his many voyages took him up the river that was later named after him. Henry Hudson died in the Arctic in 1611 while pursuing his dream of finding the fabled Northwest Passage.

Henry Hudson's ship the *Half Moon* reached the Hudson River highlands in 1609. Hudson was searching for the Northwest Passage. He often sent men ashore to explore and to communicate with the Indians. The *Half Moon* sailed up what is now the Hudson to near present-day Albany, New York.

Eighty-five years passed before Henry Hudson, the next European explorer, saw the river that would eventually carry his name. On the evening of September 2, 1609, Hudson's ship, the *Half Moon*, anchored at the river's mouth. Hudson, an Englishman, was hired by the Dutch East India Company to discover the Northwest Passage. The Dutch East India Company traded spices in Europe that its ships brought from the East Indies. If Hudson could find a passage through North America, the company's ships could more quickly return with valuable cargoes from the Indies.

Soon after the *Half Moon* anchored, Indians paddled their canoes to the ship to trade. They brought grapes, corn, bread, tobacco, as well as beaver and otter skins. Captain Hudson went ashore to return the visit. He wrote: "It is as pleasant a land as one can tread upon."

Hudson ordered the *Half Moon* to sail north up the river he called "The Great River of the Mountains." As they sailed slowly upstream, Robert Juet, a ship's officer wrote: "The land grew high. The river is full of fish." One day a large fish took four strong sailors to land it! The *Half Moon*'s crew feasted heartily that night.

Henry Hudson was impressed by the Indians he met. After visiting a large village, Hudson wrote there were crops "enough to load three ships." Juet added that they "found good ground for Corne and other Garden herbs with a great store of goodly Oakes, and Walnut trees, and Chestnut trees … and a great store of Slate for houses."

Hudson, like many European explorers, ignored Indian rights to the lands he visited. Instead, he claimed the valley of the Muhheakunnuk for the Dutch. After sailing north about 150 miles (to where Albany is today), Hudson found the river was too shallow for the *Half Moon* to proceed. A disappointed Hudson, realizing the Great River of the Mountains was not the Northwest Passage, sadly turned around.

On October 4, the *Half Moon* reached the Atlantic. Juet wrote, "We weighed [anchor] and came out of the River into which we had run so faire." Hudson never knew that one day the Great River of the Mountains would be named the Hudson in his honor.

Hudson sailed to Holland with tales of the wealth of the Hudson River valley. Eager Dutch traders ventured to New Netherland. They returned with shiploads of valuable otter, beaver, and mink furs, calling the Hudson the *Noordt,* or North, River. Before long, European colonists followed in their footsteps.

The First Colonists

In 1624 two dozen Walloon families (from French-speaking Belgium) sailed from Amsterdam, Holland, to the Noordt River. These first colonists built their homes on an island the local Mannahattes Indians called *Man Hatta*, "The Hilly Island." Because these lands were under Dutch control, the new settlers proudly called their settlement of huts "New Amsterdam" after Amsterdam, Holland. Today this is Manhattan Island.

THE SALE OF MANHATTAN ISLAND

For years, the tale was told that Dutch settlers purchased Manhattan Island from the Mannahattes Indians for only a handful of glass beads and some inexpensive trade goods. History, however, provides no documentation to prove this is how the Dutch actually gained control of Manhattan. The story began in the 1800s and is still told today. The Dutch, however, did use Indian wampum for trading. The prized wampum belts were fashioned out of special shells into unique designs.

During the 1600s, settlers from Sweden, Norway, and France filled in the riverbanks between the two growing Dutch villages—Albany along the northern Hudson and New Amsterdam at the river's mouth. Since few of these new colonists could afford to buy land, most rented their farms from the original Dutch settlers.

These early colonists clung to the Hudson's banks. They feared the surrounding wilderness away from the river. Why leave, they thought, when the river provided them with everything they needed: fresh water, unlimited fish, easy transportation, plentiful game animals, wood for fires and building, and unbelievable beauty?

The British Arrive

In 1664 five British ships sailed into New Amsterdam's harbor. At this time Great Britain and Holland were at war in Europe. Their conflict had spread to the New World and to New Netherland. The British, without firing a shot, took control of Manhattan and the entire Hudson River valley. New Netherland became New York. New Amsterdam became New York City. Other Dutch names have remained to this day: Peekskill, Brooklyn, Staten, and Tappan Zee.

The British wrote enthusiastic letters home singing the praises of the rich Hudson region. Before long, many more English families migrated to the Hudson Valley. For the next one hundred years, the colony of New York, with the Hudson at its heart, grew rapidly. New towns climbed the river's banks. Farms spread into the wilderness. Gradually, many Indians were forced to move west as European colonists took their lands.

WASHINGTON IRVING (1783–1859)

The Hudson River valley is the setting for some of America's best-known stories. Washington Irving, born in New York in the year the Revolutionary War ended, became world-famous for his eerie tales of hauntings along the Hudson. Irving based many of his tales on Dutch legends about the Hudson River. In the spooky "Legend of Sleepy Hollow," Irving's headless horseman gallops through Tarrytown. In another tale, Rip Van Winkle sleeps for twenty years and misses the Revolutionary War after bowling with miniature Dutchmen in the Catskill Mountains.

The Revolutionary War

In the 1700s many New York colonists, as well as settlers in the other twelve British colonies, wanted freedom from British rule. On July 4, 1776, the colonies declared their independence from Great Britain and formed the thirteen United States. The Revolutionary War would decide whether the United States would be a new nation or return to British rule. The Hudson River played a critical role in the outcome of the Revolutionary War.

The Hudson was the key to the British to split the colonies in two. The Hudson would become a wedge dividing New England from the rest of the rebelling colonies. The British would first defeat the colonies of New England, then the remaining colonies. The Hudson would be their river road to victory!

In 1776 the British put their plan in effect. They forced General George Washington to abandon Manhattan and give up control of the Hudson's mouth. With the port of New York in their possession, the British began their second wave of attacks. In 1777 Sir William Howe prepared to send an army up the Hudson. Sir Howe would join General Burgoyne's army marching south from Canada. Together—they planned—the two armies would successfully split the rebellious colonies.

In September 1777, Burgoyne's troops safely crossed the Hudson and gathered on its western shore near Albany. General Burgoyne's goal was to capture Albany. On his way to capture the city Burgoyne proudly proclaimed, "Britons never retreat!"

General Burgoyne never had a chance to retreat. General Washington was equally determined to control the Hudson River. Part of the American army under General Horatio Gates marched to stop Burgoyne. On October 17, 1777, General Gates defeated and captured Burgoyne's British army. The upper Hudson remained an American river for the rest of the war.

When the Revolutionary War ended in 1783, the United States was a new nation. In the treaty ending the war, the British were to give up all their land claims in North America except Canada.

Robert Fulton's steamship *Clermont* departed New York City for Albany on August 17, 1807. The *Clermont*'s voyage, the first by a steamboat in America, opened the Hudson and other river roads by providing fast, cheap, and reliable transportation.

The completion of the Erie Canal was a major event in U.S. history. By linking the waters of the Great Lakes with those of the Atlantic Ocean, the interior of America was opened for settlement. On November 4, 1825, New York governor DeWitt Clinton, a longtime supporter of the canal, poured water from Lake Erie into the Atlantic to celebrate the "Wedding of the Waters."

A modern-day replica of Henry Hudson's ship *Half Moon* anchors off Manhattan nearly four hundred years after the first *Half Moon* reached America's shores.

With the coming of peace, settlers flocked to the Hudson Valley. Many more longed for the unsettled western lands now owned by the United States, lands stretching to the Great Lakes and the Mississippi River. The towering Adirondack Mountains, however, blocked their passage west. Somehow a way had to be found through the rugged mountains.

Steamboats on the Hudson

Travel on the Hudson had long been by sail or canoe. In 1807 Robert Fulton's steamboat *Clermont* changed Hudson River travel forever. Sparks flying, engine chugging, paddle wheels splashing, the *Clermont* proudly announced its historic arrival on the river. One frightened man said the *Clermont* was like a fire-breathing, smoke-belching water monster.

Soon other steamboats made travel on the Hudson faster and cheaper. But the steamboats could carry people and products only as far as Albany. The rugged wall of the Adirondack Mountains blocked their passage.

Early explorers had followed the fast-flowing Mohawk River through the mountains north and west of Albany. *Could this route be the gateway to the west?* settlers wondered. *How could they carry their possessions over such a difficult passage?*

To reach the West in those days, a traveler had to sail up the Hudson, unload his goods, and load them onto a cart. The cart rumbled along rough roads to the calmer Mohawk waters past Schenectady. There, the traveler unloaded his cart, loaded his things onto another boat, and continued his journey. Such travel was difficult, exhausting, and expensive. The unloading and loading were repeated when the Mohawk grew too rugged. There were dense forests, swamps, and other barriers to cross until the weary traveler finally reached Lake Erie. Once on Lake Erie, however, he had clear sailing into the middle of America.

The Erie Canal

Many people thought building a canal linking the Hudson River to Lake Erie was a foolish idea. No one had ever before built a four-hundred-mile-long canal!

But the idea of a canal to Lake Erie wouldn't die. Many people, led by New York governor DeWitt Clinton, believed a canal connecting the Hudson River to Lake Erie was possible. Clinton was convinced that if farmers and shopkeepers had access to land west of the Appalachians, the whole country could prosper. Clinton worked doggedly to get others to believe in his dream.

Clinton's followers walked suggested routes. They hired engineers to examine the rocks, soils, hills, and swamps along the way. They sent surveyors to map the lakes and streams that a canal could connect for easy westward passage.

In 1825, after years of backbreaking work and clever engineering, the Erie Canal opened. On November 4 of that year, Governor Clinton poured two barrels of freshwater from Lake Erie into the Atlantic's salty waters. The Lake Erie water had been carried aboard the *Seneca Chief* through the Erie Canal and down the Hudson River. Cannons fired, folks cheered, and bells rang when the two waters mingled for the first time. The entire country celebrated this historic "Wedding of the Waters." Our first major river road was open!

Low bridge, everybody down!
Low bridge for we're comin' to a town!
And you'll always know your neighbor,
You'll always know your pal,
If you've ever navigated on the Erie Canal.
—Chorus of traditional American folk song
   (see page 6)

The Erie Canal linked the Hudson and the Great Lakes, opening the heart of the continent to settlement. The trickle of settlers and goods heading west quickly became a flood. Immigrants from Europe now sailed across the Atlantic, steamed up the Hudson, rode a canal boat to Lake Erie, and set sail again with their feet rarely touching land! Farms and towns prospered along the Erie Canal. Settlements, and then later cities, spread along the shores of Lake Erie, Lake Huron, Lake Michigan, and Lake Superior. The combination of the Hudson River and the 363-mile-long Erie Canal quickly became the most popular and important river road west.

From a tiny brook flowing from a mountain pond, the Hudson made history happen. Today major truck and train routes follow much of the path pioneered by the Erie Canal. Canoes and boats still ply her waters. The Hudson remains as busy as ever. Ferries scuttle back and forth, sailboats race, barges surge, and ships unload their international cargoes as the Hudson continues to be an invaluable American river.

Ohio River at Cincinnati

Question: What river is round at both ends

    and high in the middle?

Answer: The O-HI-O!

—Children's riddle

The boatman is a lucky man,

No one can do as the boatman can.

The boatmen dance and the boatmen sing,

The boatman is up to everything.

Hi-O, away we go.

Floating down the river on the O-hi-o!

—Traditional rhyme recited by children
  floating on flatboats on the Ohio

The Ohio

The Ohio Begins

When does one river plus one river equal one river? When the Monongahela River combines with the Allegheny River to make the Ohio River!

On a map of the United States it is easy to pinpoint where the Ohio River begins: at the tip of the peninsula where Pittsburgh stands today. From this point, the Ohio winds 981 miles through America's magnificent heartland.

Sometimes, the rolling river twists and turns as if it can't decide which direction to flow. The Ohio flows first northwest, curves southwest, turns west, and shifts southwest again. But no matter which direction the river runs, the Ohio has been a predominant river road west.

ADDING TO THE OHIO

From Pittsburgh to its mouth at Cairo, Illinois, the Ohio River borders five states: West Virginia, Ohio, Indiana, Kentucky, and Illinois. However, the Ohio drains water from fourteen states. The Beaver, Duck, Big Sandy, Licking, Scioto, Great Miami, Wabash, Rolling Fork, White Oak, Cumberland, and Tennessee rivers all contribute their waters to the Ohio. Every second, the Ohio pours two million gallons of water into the Mississippi! With the addition of the Ohio's water, the Mississippi River (already joined upstream by the Missouri) becomes the largest and longest of America's rivers.

The Ohio Forms

More than twelve thousand years ago, massive glaciers determined the Ohio's convoluted course. The towering glaciers blocked rivers from flowing north. The rivers were forced to run south and west. In doing so, these ancient rivers created the course the future Ohio would follow. As they melted, the glaciers released tremendous

amounts of water, further forming the Ohio's riverbed. The retreating glaciers shaped the surrounding lands, leaving behind rolling hills covered with a deep layer of fertile soil.

Indians Find a Beautiful Land and a Great River

An immense variety of animals and plants spread throughout the Ohio Valley after the glaciers disappeared. Around twelve thousand years ago, Indians settling in the Ohio Valley found flourishing forests of maple, hickory, sycamore, dogwood, and beech. The Indians hunted deer, bear, wolf, beaver, moose, mink, otter, fox, squirrels, ducks, geese, cranes, turkeys, and pigeons. Buffalo, grazing on open grasslands, were a ready source of meat and skins. The Indians caught walleye, trout, and bass in the rippling Ohio. Wild plants, in addition to crops of corn, beans, and squash, supplied them with more food.

The bountiful region became home for the Miami, Shawnee, and Illinois Indians. They built their villages throughout the valley. The Iroquois, who hunted in the area, named the rippling Ohio "Great River."

OHIO VALLEY MOUNDS

The Indians left enduring evidence of their long habitation of the Ohio Valley. Native peoples, whom archaeologists call the Adena and Hopewell cultures, built thousands of earth and stone mounds. The earliest mounds were constructed for burials three thousand years ago. Many of these mounds were shaped like turtles, bears, foxes, birds, lizards, and men. Other mounds were circles, squares, and rectangles. Some impressive mounds remain today. Grave Creek Mound in West Virginia stands about seventy feet tall. Great Serpent Mound in Ohio winds its way for thirteen hundred feet before opening its gigantic jaws to swallow an enormous earthen egg.

An Indian River Road

The Ohio was an important river road for the Indians. They traveled in canoes to hunt, visit relatives, or go to war. They followed the Ohio's many tributaries far into the interior forests and prairies. Millions of human and animal feet etched trails into the Ohio's banks and through the forests. This network of water and land trails linked villages hundreds of miles apart.

The Ohio River was part of a widespread Indian trading network. Shells from the Gulf Coast and copper from the Great Lakes were traded along the Ohio. Arrowheads chipped from obsidian, a black volcanic

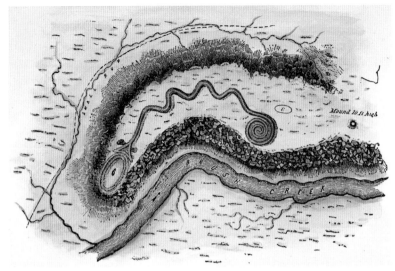

LEFT TO RIGHT

The Monongahela and Allegheny rivers meet at the tip of a peninsula in southwestern Pennsylvania to form the Ohio River. This peninsula was vital to European interests in North America. The French and British fought over this junction. Many American traders and families headed down the Ohio from this point. Today, the thriving city of Pittsburgh stands at the Ohio's beginning.

Indians in the Ohio Valley built hundreds of earthen mounds. One of these, the Great Serpent Mound in southern Ohio, is thirteen hundred feet long. Visitors today can climb a tower and marvel at the artistry of this effigy mound.

glass found in the Rocky Mountains, have been discovered in Ohio burial sites.

The Indians enjoyed, explored, and prospered in the Ohio Valley for more than twelve thousand years before European adventurers entered the region.

The Arrival of the Europeans

Who was the first European to gaze upon the Ohio's sparkling waters? History does not tell us. The Indians told the French, the Dutch, and the English about a beautiful river on the western side of the Appalachians. The European explorers hoped the Ohio was the fabled Northwest Passage leading to the riches of Asia.

Interest in the Ohio River region became more intense in 1662 when Father Lalemant, a French priest in Montreal, Canada, wrote about the large Indian villages "stretched along a Beautiful River which serves to carry people down to the Great Lake (the ocean) where they trade with Europeans."

RELIGION, EXPLORATION, AND ECONOMICS TRAVELED HAND IN HAND

In the 1600s many French Canadian explorers were Jesuit priests determined to bring the Catholic religion to the Indians. Other adventuresome explorers and traders often joined the fearless priests venturing into the western wilderness.

The explorers did so to claim new lands for France and, with luck, discover the Northwest Passage. Traders carried pots, kettles, pans, blankets, knives, buttons, axes, and traps to the Indians in exchange for thick fox, beaver, muskrat, and mink furs. The fur trade became increasingly important to the Indian economy. By trading with Europeans, the Indians received metal tools and cooking utensils, woven cloth, glass beads, guns, and gunpowder, which they could not make themselves.

René-Robert La Salle, French Explorer

René-Robert Cavelier, Sieur de La Salle, was one of the most famous French explorers. La Salle had such an intense interest in finding a route to China that he dressed in colorful Chinese robes. His companions called him *La Chine*, "the Chinese."

La Salle left Montreal in 1669 to find the Ohio River, explore it, and claim the land for France. The French

Colonel George Washington and his militia took control of Fort Duquesne from the French in November 1758. British soldiers raised their flag over the fort they rebuilt and named it Fort Pitt. Pittsburgh, at the beginning of the Ohio River, is named after Fort Pitt.

already claimed much of Canada and were attempting to expand their North American empire.

Soon after crossing Lake Ontario, however, La Salle fell ill. He was forced to spend the winter recovering far from his Ohio River goal. During his recovery, La Salle met Louis Joliet, another French explorer. La Salle questioned Joliet about his discoveries. La Salle was especially eager for news about the river the French called *La Belle Rivière*, "The Beautiful River"—the Ohio.

The British Enter the Ohio Valley

By the late 1600s the British had learned about the Ohio from the Indians who had shared their enthusiasm for the region's bounty. Trappers and traders soon ventured into the Ohio Valley. The British planned to establish colonies, take command of the rich fur trade, and prevent the French from expanding their North American empire.

Competition between the French and British for the Indian fur trade intensified in the mid-1700s. The Ohio had become the centerpiece in the struggle between France and Great Britain to dominate North America.

To defend their Ohio claims from the British, the French built Forts Presque Isle, LeBoeuf, and Venango between Lake Erie and the Ohio River.

Not to be outmaneuvered, the British decided to build forts of their own in the Ohio country. In 1753 a young Virginia colonist named George Washington was sent to see if the triangle of land where the Allegheny and Monongahela rivers met was suitable for a fort. Washington wrote that the land "was extremely well situated for a Fort; as it has the absolute Command of both Rivers."

Washington also carried a British message to the French demanding that they leave the Ohio region. The French ignored the threat. They were planning to build a fort in the spring of 1754 at the forks where the Ohio River began. But the British beat them to it, creating a small fort in early April at the site Washington had selected. Later that month, a large French army forced the British to surrender their fort and built one in the same place. They named it Fort Duquesne in honor of Marquis Duquesne, governor-general of New France, the name for lands claimed by the French in North America.

George Washington Begins a War

George Washington was ordered back to Ohio in the spring of 1754, this time to capture Fort Duquesne. Near the fort, Washington attacked and defeated a small French force. After this, his first battle, Washington wrote, "I heard Bulletts whistle and believe me there was something charming in the sound." These bullets were the opening shots in the French and Indian War.

Before long, however, Washington heard more bullets than even he wanted to. The angry French surprised Washington and defeated him in a bloody battle (no doubt

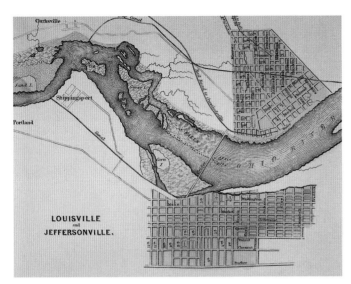

The Falls of the Ohio provided a natural stopping place for travelers on the Ohio River. Louisville, Kentucky (bottom), and Jeffersonville, Indiana (top), grew on opposite sides of the river at the falls to help river traffic.

the bullets weren't so charming to him this time). George Washington surrendered his men in early July 1754.

The French and Indian War raged across the frontier for the next nine years. The war ended in 1763 with a British victory. France was forced to give its North American empire to Britain. England now controlled Canada as well as the lands stretching west from the Atlantic seaboard to the Mississippi. The Ohio River valley was in British hands—but not for long.

To oversee their Ohio lands, the British built Fort Pitt on the site of Fort Duquesne, which was destroyed in the war. Fort Pitt was named in honor of William Pitt, the British prime minister who had led the British to victory in the war. With the war's end, hundreds of British settlers built homes and shops around Fort Pitt. They named their rapidly growing town Pittsburgh.

The Revolutionary War

After the end of the war, the British faced a new struggle, this one with her thirteen American colonies. The British wanted the Americans to pay for the French and Indian War, so they taxed the colonists for part of the war's cost.

But the American colonists disagreed with that decision, arguing that it was unfair for them to be taxed by Britain since they had no voice in establishing taxes. Tensions between the thirteen colonies and Britain exploded in April 1775, when the Revolutionary War erupted in Massachusetts. That summer the Continental Congress gave command of America's armies to General Washington, who had gained his military and leadership skills on the Ohio frontier.

Victory in the Revolutionary War in 1783 gave the new United States its independence. In the Treaty of Paris ending the war, the United States took over all British lands from the Atlantic to the Mississippi River, including the Ohio River valley. In less than twenty years the flags of three nations had flown over the Ohio River: French, British, and American.

American Pioneers Fill the Ohio Valley

After peace was declared, American pioneers seeking new homes in the Ohio wilderness poured over the Appalachians. Many settlers journeyed overland to Pittsburgh in wagons, on horseback, and on foot. Some bought boats or built rafts to float down the Ohio River highway.

Many pioneers traveled partway down the Ohio before heading up her numerous tributaries. They carved farms out of the wilderness in the future states of Ohio, Kentucky, Indiana, and Illinois. Others settled in prosperous young towns like Cincinnati, Wheeling, and Louisville.

Louisville, a natural stopping place at the Falls of the Ohio, grew rapidly. Each year hundreds of flatboats

John Chapman, better known as Johnny Appleseed, was a familiar face on the Ohio River in the early nineteenth century as he planted his apple seeds. Pioneers traveling down the Ohio greatly appreciated Johnny's efforts. Appleseed, who lived from 1774 to 1845, became one of America's best-loved folk heroes.

and keelboats stopped at Louisville. These boats were loaded with products grown or made in the Ohio region: flour, pork, cider, soap, rope, beans, onions, butter, beef, cheese, cloth, corn, potatoes, bacon, horses, chickens, lumber, boots, saddles, pots, kettles, pottery, venison, and whiskey.

The Ohio Valley proved to be rich in natural resources, too. Coal was mined in Pennsylvania, West Virginia, Ohio, and Kentucky. Salt for preserving food was discovered in Kentucky. Limestone for building and for forging iron was plentiful.

THE LINCOLNS, AN OHIO VALLEY PIONEER FAMILY

Thomas Lincoln, an Ohio pioneer, farmed in northern Kentucky at Sinking Spring Farm. There, on February 12, 1809, his son Abraham was born. When Abe was seven, his family ferried across the Ohio to farm in Indiana. There they lived in a rough cabin not far from the Ohio River.

After visiting his Indiana home in 1844, Abe wrote a poem about his early Indiana days. He called it "The Bear Hunt."

When first my father settled here,
'Twas then the frontier line:
The panther's scream, filled night with fear
And bears preyed on the swine.

The Ohio Becomes a River Road West

The Ohio became an increasingly busy river road during the early 1800s. Families loaded flatboats with farm animals, food, and tools and floated downstream searching for a better life.

Telling tales and singing songs made the long days and nights aboard a flatboat pass more quickly. "The Banks of the Pleasant Ohio," written by an unknown balladeer, was one of the most popular pioneer songs.

Come all young men who have a mind for to range,
Into the western country your station to change,
For seeking some new pleasures we'll altogether go,
And we'll settle on the banks of the pleasant Ohio.

Traveling on the river was not all fun. The pioneers faced frequent dangers. Sudden storms damaged their fragile crafts. Hidden rocks and snags sank them. Rafts ran aground or wrecked in fog as thick as soup. Surging floods swamped them. River pirates attacked them. But still the determined pioneers pressed on.

Mike Fink was a rough, tough, loudmouthed, but exceptionally skilled keelboatman. Mike's reputation reached far beyond the Ohio Valley, and his feats on and off the Ohio River became legendary.

JOHNNY APPLESEED

John Chapman, better known as Johnny Appleseed, traveled west on the Ohio. Johnny paddled a canoe full of apple seeds down the river in 1806. Along the way he planted his precious apple seeds. When he ran out of seeds, Johnny hiked back to Pittsburgh, gathered more seeds, and set out to spread his orchards. When pioneers arrived, they found apples galore growing for them!

Ohio Keelboats Carried More Than Cargo

Professional rivermen took heavily loaded keelboats downstream from Pittsburgh to New Orleans, where they sold their goods. The hardy rivermen then poled, sailed, and pulled their keelboats upstream against the currents of the Mississippi and Ohio back to Pittsburgh for a new load. Some keelboaters, reluctant to pole back upstream, sold their crafts in New Orleans for lumber. With their pay in their pockets they walked back north along the Natchez Trace through Mississippi, Tennessee, and Kentucky to the Ohio Valley. Robbers often lurked along the trace, making this a hazardous journey.

Mike Fink became one of the most famous of the keelboaters. Born around 1770 in Pittsburgh, Mike spent his early life on the Ohio River. Over the years he became famous not only for his keelboating skills but also for his practical jokes, eagerness to fight, and bragging.

Meriwether Lewis and William Clark were two other famous adventurers who journeyed on the Ohio. Lewis and Clark began their famous expedition together across America at the Falls of the Ohio on the other side of the river from Louisville. In 1803, in a keelboat built in Pittsburgh, they headed down the Ohio, gathering the men and supplies needed to venture across a continent.

Steamboat 'Round the Bend!

The quiet of the Ohio River was shattered in 1811 by a steamboat's shrieking whistle. Robert Fulton's successful Hudson River steamboat opened America's rivers to faster transportation. Nicholas Roosevelt, together with his friend and business partner Fulton, built the *New Orleans*, the first steamboat on western waters.

Roosevelt's goal was to take his steamboat almost fifteen hundred miles from Pittsburgh to New Orleans. On October 20, 1811, sparks flew as the boat's boilers got up a head of steam. With a piercing blast of his whistle, Roosevelt steered the *New Orleans* into the Ohio. Roosevelt's wife, Lydia, young daughter Rosetta,

The Ohio River played a central role in the Underground Railroad. Once fugitive slaves crossed the river, they were in the Free States of Ohio, Indiana, and Illinois. This crossing place was located on the river at Steubenville, Ohio.

Bridges across the Ohio became increasingly important in the nineteenth century as more people settled in the Ohio Valley. The bridges had to be strong enough to withstand raging spring floods and to carry locomotives and their heavily loaded cars. The coming of the railroads spelled the end of much of the steamboat traffic on the Ohio.

and their big black dog Tiger joined him on this river adventure. All along the way, people gathered to watch the *New Orleans* steam downstream. When the glowing, fiery *New Orleans* reached Louisville in the middle of the night, the surprised townspeople thought a comet had exploded over their town!

On January 10, 1812, the *New Orleans* steamed into New Orleans, having survived low water, terrible storms, and an earthquake. Roosevelt had opened both the Ohio and the Mississippi rivers to steam travel!

River Road to Freedom
The Ohio River, the river road west for many free Americans, was also a river road to freedom for many African Americans.

In 1787 Congress had passed the Northwest Ordinance, outlining how the Ohio region would be settled. Slavery would not be allowed north of the Ohio River, the boundary between the slaveholding states of the South and the free states of the North. Thousands of slaves lived in Kentucky and Virginia (West Virginia became a separate state during the Civil War).

The 350 miles of river bordering Kentucky and western Virginia became a major route to freedom for hundreds of slaves. In the years before the Civil War, many slaves from the South made desperate crossings of the Ohio to freedom in the North. They were aided to freedom by free African Americans as well as sympathetic white men and women along the Underground Railroad, which was not really a railroad but a network of stations where slaves found help on their way north.

Runaway slaves, most of whom had never been taught to read, often used traditional songs like "Follow the Drinkin' Gourd" to guide them north to freedom. The drinkin' gourd was the Big Dipper constellation hanging in the sky, pointing to the North Star, pointing to freedom. The song's words told runaway slaves of the route north to the Ohio River. Once across the Ohio, the slaves were free.

Where the river ends in between two hills
Follow the drinkin' gourd.
There the Ole Man's waitin' for to carry you to freedom.
Follow the drinkin' gourd.

The Civil War
When he was twenty-two years old, Abraham Lincoln floated down the Ohio and Mississippi rivers to New Orleans. His flatboat was loaded with salted meat, barrels, lumber, and live hogs. Lincoln saw a slave market in New Orleans, a sight that changed his life. After watching black slaves being ruthlessly bought and sold, according to legend Lincoln wrote, "If I ever get a chance to hit that thing [slavery], I'll hit it hard."

Later, during the Civil War, President Lincoln issued the Emancipation Proclamation on January 1, 1863. The Emancipation Proclamation declared "that all persons held as slaves" within the rebelling Southern states "are, and henceforward shall be free."

The End of an Era

River traffic on the Ohio began to dwindle after the Civil War. The money and effort put into the war were now channeled into other ventures. One of these was the transcontinental railroad linking the Atlantic to the Pacific. With its completion on May 10, 1869, people and products could travel quickly and cheaply. Pittsburgh, with access to coal and iron, became the steel-producing hub of America. Engines, boxcars, and steel rails rolled out of its fiery furnaces.

By the late 1800s fewer and fewer flatboats and keelboats drifted downstream. The expanding—and less expensive—railroads carried more and more people and products. Fertile farms covered the lands where Indians had lived and the forest flourished. Mike Fink and Johnny Appleseed had become characters in stories told around kitchen stoves and in front of comfortable fireplaces. Gone were the days of children shouting, "Steamboat 'round the bend!" The Ohio's heyday had passed, but its role as an invaluable river road west will be remembered.

No bottom.

Mark four.

Quarter less four.

Half twain.

Quarter twain.

Quarter less four.

Half twain.

Quarter twain.

Mark twain.

— In the 1800s the leadsman aboard a steamboat called out the changing depths of the Mississippi River to the pilot so he would know the safest place to steer. "Mark twain" was the safe depth for a Mississippi steamboat.

The great Mississippi, the majestic, the magnificent

Mississippi, rolling its mile-wide tide along,

shining in the sun

— Mark Twain, American author and Mississippi River pilot (1835–1910)

The Mississippi

Lake Itasca, the True Headwaters

On July 13, 1832, the scientist and explorer Henry Rowe Schoolcraft climbed a hill in northern Minnesota. Schoolcraft gazed down upon a small Y-shaped lake. A narrow stream meandering out of the lake disappeared into the surrounding forest. Schoolcraft excitedly wrote: "What had been long sought at last appeared suddenly. On turning out of a thicket, into a small weedy opening, the cheering sight of a transparent body of water burst upon our view. It was Itasca lake, the source of the Mississippi."

Schoolcraft created the name Itasca from two Latin words: "Itas" from ver*ITAS* ("truth") and "Ca" from *CAput* ("head")—Lake Itasca, the true headwaters of the Mississippi.

Winding out of Lake Itasca, the Mississippi is shallow enough and narrow enough to wade across, and it moves at one mile an hour. You can easily walk faster than that! More than 2,500 miles later and over a mile wide in places, the mighty Mississippi reaches the Gulf of Mexico.

The Mississippi has had many names: *Messipi, Missi Sepe, Gichi-ziibi, Ne Tongo, Chucagua, Tamalisen, Ri, Mamese-Sipou,* Colbert, The Lost River, Father of Waters, Gathering of Waters, *Rio de Espiritu Santo,* Muddy Mississippi, Mighty Mississippi, *El Grande*, Ol' Man River, Big Muddy, Big River, and Great River.

Mississippi—from the Ojibwa word *Misi-ziibi,* "Great River"—is the name echoing down the centuries for America's most vital river.

The mighty Mississippi River begins as a trickle leaving Lake Itasca in Minnesota. Many explorers looked for the Mississippi's headwaters until it was found and named by Henry Schoolcraft in 1832. From the lake, the Mississippi rolls more than 2,500 miles to the Gulf of Mexico.

At its peak, Cahokia (top), near the Mississippi River, was the largest Indian community north of Mexico. Monks Mound towered over Cahokia's central plaza, which was surrounded by a defensive log wall. Homes, ceremonial centers, fields, ponds, and streams completed the vast complex of Cahokia where ten to twenty thousand people once lived.

Monks Mound (bottom), the largest prehistoric structure in North America, stands one hundred feet high.

De Soto was the first European to see the Mississippi River, but no one is sure exactly where he saw it. In this painting by William H. Powell, de Soto meets with Indians before building boats to cross the mighty river.

In 1673 the French explorers Marquette and Joliet left the mouth of the Wisconsin River and paddled onto the Mississippi. Marquette and Joliet carefully recorded their journey. Their reports spurred further French exploration of the Mississippi Valley.

THE MIGHTY MISSISSIPPI

From its headwaters to its mouth at the Gulf of Mexico, the Mississippi flows more than 2,552 miles, making it the longest river in North America. A drop of rain falling in Lake Itasca journeys ninety days before reaching the Gulf. The Mississippi and its tributaries drain almost half of the United States, gathering waters from thirty-one states in addition to two Canadian provinces. No wonder the Mississippi is nicknamed the "Mighty Mississippi"!

The Mississippi, the Indians' River Road

For thousands of years Indians used the Mississippi as a river road through their homelands. The Sioux, Ojibwa, Illinois, Fox, Sauk, Kickapoo, Chickasaw, Choctaw, Natchez, Chitimacha, Iowa, Missouri, Dakota, and other tribes paddled their canoes and fished on the river. Numerous deer, bear, buffalo, beaver, geese, ducks, muskrats, and swans lived along its shores and wetlands. Annual floods from melting spring snow deposited rich soils for bean, corn, squash, sunflower, and pumpkin crops. Broad forests supplied fuel for fires, building materials, nuts, and berries as well as habitats for mammals and birds. Indian villages, large and small, prospered along or near the Mississippi.

The Mississippi was a convenient river highway for the Indians who traded such local resources as shells, flint, copper, and seeds. Their trading network extended from the Gulf of Mexico up the Mississippi to Minnesota, up the Missouri to the Rocky Mountains, and up the Ohio to the Alleghenies.

Cahokia, Prehistoric America's Amazing City

Cahokia (situated opposite what is now St. Louis) was the largest Indian city ever built north of Mexico. At its peak around the year AD 1200, ten to twenty thousand people lived in the Cahokia community, which covered five square miles, and as many more in the several surrounding villages and towns. Cahokia was thriving for five hundred years before Europeans reached America's shores.

Cahokia's builders had wisely chosen a location where Mississippi River floods could seldom reach them, fertile soils were abundant, and nearby forests could furnish plentiful wood. Cahokia stood on the Mississippi's eastern floodplain with easy access upstream to the Missouri and downstream to the Ohio. Many major Indian trade routes crossed there, providing the Cahokians markets for their products and goods to receive in trade from as far away as Florida and Minnesota.

Cahokia's most outstanding features were its earthen mounds. More than 80 of the original 120 mounds still exist from the time when Cahokia was at its peak. Monks Mound, the largest prehistoric earth structure in North America, stands one hundred feet high. Some mounds were for burials, but most mounds were for ceremonies and

celebrations for the living. Archaeologists think Cahokia's leaders lived in large houses and on mounds inside the wooden walls surrounding the central ceremonial precinct. The rest of the community lived in homes and farms outside Cahokia's walled district.

For some unknown reason, the vast city of Cahokia was abandoned before AD 1400. A little more than one hundred years later, European explorers reached America's shores, bringing changes across the continent but never seeing Cahokia in its glory.

The Spanish See the Mississippi

In 1541 Hernando de Soto, a Spanish explorer, was the first European to see the Mississippi's muddy waters. De Soto had marched from Florida with more than six hundred men. His goal was to claim land for Spain and to gain riches, especially gold, for himself. De Soto and his companions had wandered for two years through what is now Florida, North Carolina, South Carolina, Tennessee, Georgia, Alabama, and Mississippi before reaching the Mississippi. No one is exactly sure where de Soto first saw the Mississippi. Memphis, Tennessee, and Tunica, Mississippi, are the most likely places.

De Soto called the big river *el Rio Grande*, "the Big River," and claimed it for Spain. After more wanderings west of the Mississippi, de Soto's luck ran out—he died. His men sank his body into the Mississippi's swirling waters.

Marquette and Joliet Paddle down the Mississippi

More than one hundred years later, in 1673, the French explorers Father Marquette and Louis Joliet ventured upon the Mississippi. They paddled from Canada in birchbark canoes through the Great Lakes to the Wisconsin River. Their mission was to claim land for France and convert Indians to the Catholic religion.

The Menominees of Wisconsin told the explorers about the "Big Water," the *Missi Sepe,* to the west. Marquette and Joliet hoped this Missi Sepe was the fabled Northwest Passage leading to Asia. Eager to find out, the men reached the misty Mississippi on June 17, 1673.

Marquette described his first view of the Mississippi: "Behold us, then, upon this celebrated river.... Its channel is very narrow at the mouth of the Mesconsin [Wisconsin River], and runs south until it is affected by very high hills. Its current is slow."

Marquette and Joliet paddled south seeking the Mississippi's mouth. They hunted deer and buffalo, fished, spent time with the Indians they met, and became the first Europeans to see the Missouri River. Marquette and Joliet continued south until they reached the mouth of the Arkansas River. Marquette recorded: "We judged by the compass, that the Mississippi discharged itself into the Gulf of Mexico. … Having satisfied ourselves … , we resolved to return home."

LaSalle Claiming Louisiana for France by George Catlin. On April 9, 1682, the French explorer La Salle planted a cross and a lead plaque near the mouth of the Mississippi River, claiming the entire Mississippi Valley and beyond for France. He named this vast territory "Louisiana" to honor the French king Louis XIV.

In 1803 the United States purchased Louisiana from France, doubling the size of the country. With hundreds of ships from around the world sailing to New Orleans every year, the city grew and rapidly became one of America's most important ports.

La Salle Claims and Names Louisiana

French explorer René-Robert de La Salle was fascinated with Joliet's tales of the Mississippi. Earlier, La Salle had tried to find the Ohio but failed. La Salle decided to travel all the way down the Mississippi to its mouth. He planned to claim the entire Mississippi River valley for King Louis XIV of France, who was expanding his North American empire. La Salle and his companions raced down the Mississippi, claiming both sides of the Mississippi for France. La Salle finally stopped when he reached the Mississippi's mouth.

There, on April 9, 1682, La Salle planted a cross and a marker to establish France's right to the lands through which he had passed. La Salle declared that all "the seas, harbors, ports, bays, adjacent straits and all the nations, people, provinces, cities, towns, villages, mines, minerals, fisheries, streams, and rivers" now belonged to King Louis XIV. In one brief statement, La Salle claimed the entire Mississippi River system from the Gulf of Mexico to the Rocky Mountains, a region larger than France itself!

La Salle named this vast land "Louisiana" to honor King Louis XIV. Louisiana, Missouri, Arkansas, Iowa, Minnesota, Kansas, Nebraska, Colorado, North Dakota, South Dakota, Montana, Wyoming, and Oklahoma would eventually be created from "Louisiana."

The Spanish Return

The French established New Orleans to control Louisiana. The small village, which became the capital of Louisiana in 1718, was the key to the French empire in America. France, however, gave up Louisiana and New Orleans in 1763 when France lost the French and Indian War. Spain, an ally of victorious Britain in the war, received Louisiana.

The Spanish governed the Mississippi Valley for the next forty years. They profited from the growing number of American farmers settling west of the Appalachian Mountains. By 1790 more than two hundred thousand settlers lived in the Mississippi Valley. These pioneers shipped their products down the Mississippi to New Orleans. In New Orleans the goods were put aboard ships sailing to Europe. New Orleans became increasingly important to Spain, France, and the developing United States because whoever owned New Orleans controlled commerce on the Mississippi.

The Louisiana Purchase

In 1802 France reappeared in the Mississippi picture. Napoleon, soon to be emperor of France, wished to regain his nation's lost American empire. To accomplish this, Napoleon made a secret deal with Spain to obtain Louisiana. Napoleon gave Spain several valuable Italian regions that France owned in exchange for Louisiana.

THE VALUE OF THE MISSISSIPPI RIVER

By the early 1800s, three out of every eight bushels of corn grown by American farmers were shipped to market on the Mississippi. Half of America's marketable hogs were shipped through New Orleans. Fifty percent of the furs sent to Europe traveled down the Mississippi. Flour, cotton, horses, tobacco, cattle, and apples also were shipped through New Orleans. The products sold, bought, and delivered were worth tens of millions of dollars. As New Orleans grew, the city's motto became Under My Wings Every Thing Prospers. President Jefferson wanted that prosperity under America's wings.

Spain, wary of growing American power and unable to defend Louisiana, readily agreed to the transfer.

The rapidly expanding United States also wished to possess the Mississippi. President Thomas Jefferson knew that shipping on the river was critical to the economy of the young country. If a foreign power owned New Orleans, it could stop American shipping at any time. Jefferson wrote: "There is on the globe one single spot, the possessor of which is our natural and habitual enemy. It is New Orleans, through which the produce of three eighths of our territory must pass to market."

Napoleon had his own worries. In his eagerness to conquer Europe, he had spent immense sums of money on his military. Even though he had so recently succeeded in regaining Louisiana, Napoleon could not afford to fight America to keep it.

Sensing Napoleon's predicament, President Jefferson offered to buy New Orleans from France. Napoleon completely surprised the United States by offering to sell all of Louisiana for fifteen million dollars! Jefferson couldn't pass up this bargain. For about four cents an acre (actual cost) the United States purchased Louisiana's more than 500 million acres in 1803. The Louisiana Purchase immediately doubled the size of the United States.

To learn what the United States had bought, President Jefferson then sent Meriwether Lewis and William Clark on their history-making exploration up the Missouri River.

An All-American River Highway

With the Mississippi firmly in the hands of the United States, the river's importance increased. After the Erie Canal opened in 1825, travel from New York City to the Great Lakes became possible. A system of canals connected the Great Lakes to the Ohio River. Another canal linked Lake Michigan to the Mississippi. River transportation, entirely within the United States, was now open from New York City to New Orleans.

Steamboats Rolling on the River

Before the days of the steamboats, traveling downstream on the Mississippi was fairly easy. River crafts drifted along on the steady current. The people steering the keelboats and rafts, however, had to be on constant watch for snags and islands, and deadly fog could threaten any trip. Giant eddies captured boats, spinning them like tops. Sawyers—whole trees that had fallen from a riverbank and become anchored in the river's bottom—were dangerous underwater obstacles. The sawyers seesawed up and down, ripping open any boat unlucky enough to come upon one.

This nineteenth-century Currier and Ives print shows the levee, or landing place, at New Orleans on the Mississippi River.

Abraham Lincoln worked on a flatboat that traveled down the Mississippi to New Orleans when he was a young man. Lincoln saw a slave auction in New Orleans, which strongly influenced his feelings against slavery.

Traveling upstream meant poling against the Mississippi's mighty current. This work was so hard that one Frenchman wrote: "One might as well try to bite a slice off the moon."

River travel on the Mississippi dramatically changed with the coming of the steamboat in 1811. The distinction of being the first steamboat on the Mississippi River belongs to the *New Orleans,* also the first steamboat on the Ohio. After navigating the Ohio, the *New Orleans* steamed into history on the Mississippi when it lowered its gangplank at New Orleans on January 10, 1812. Despite the hardships, dangers, earthquakes, and adventures, the maiden voyage of the *New Orleans* was a success. It had turned the Mississippi into a true river road running through the middle of America.

THE NEW MADRID EARTHQUAKE

When Nicholas Roosevelt set forth on the *New Orleans*, he had no idea what danger lurked downstream. On December 16, 1811, a monstrous earthquake struck New Madrid, Missouri, a village on the Mississippi's banks. The strong earthquake rang bells in Boston more than a thousand miles away and forced the Mississippi to actually run backward! Aboard the *New Orleans*, however, the quake felt like a slight bump.

As the *New Orleans* churned downstream, signs of the quake's destruction were everywhere. Uprooted trees had toppled into the river. Old islands had disappeared. New islands appeared. Families, their homes destroyed, were surviving in makeshift camps along the river's caving banks. Bodies of dead people and animals floated in the churning current. There was nothing Roosevelt could do to help because he had no extra room on board.

Within ten years, hundreds of steamboats paddled their way up and down the Mississippi. People and products moved swiftly from place to place. The city of New Orleans grew rapidly. By 1840 New Orleans was the fourth-largest port in the world, competing with mighty New York to handle the nation's commerce. That year, two thousand steamboats docked in New Orleans, carrying cargo worth more than fifty million dollars.

Not everyone traveled willingly on the Mississippi. Many African American slaves were forced to be on the river. Slaves stoked the fiery boilers on steamboats, loaded and unloaded cargo, and cared for passengers. Some African Americans were brave slaves who had run away from their owners, been captured, and sold to new masters down the river. Being "sold downriver" meant being sent down the Mississippi into the deep South, where escape to freedom in the North was nearly impossible.

Steamboat races were popular on the Mississippi. One of the most famous races was between the *Robert E. Lee* and the *Natchez*. Both steamboats churned north from New Orleans, but the *Lee* reached St. Louis far ahead of the *Natchez*, steaming 1,200 miles to victory.

During the Civil War, the steamboat *Sultana* transported Union troops on the Mississippi. On April 27, 1865, the *Sultana* accidentally exploded, killing more than fifteen hundred soldiers on their way home from battle.

Mark Twain grew up along the Mississippi River in Hannibal, Missouri. His books about the Mississippi brought him worldwide fame.

Be good + you will be lonesome.
Mark Twain

Danger on the River

Travel by steamboat was faster but not always safer. Fire was a constant danger. In order to be fast, early steamboats were built of light wood, which easily burst into flames from sparks flying out of the boats' chimneys. Steam boilers, used to power the paddle wheels, sometimes blew up, killing passengers and sinking vessels.

The worst steamboat disaster occurred on April 27, 1865. More than 2,500 people were aboard the *Sultana*. Most were Union soldiers returning home from the Civil War. Just after passing Paddy's Hen and Chicken islands near Memphis, the *Sultana* exploded. Despite valiant rescue attempts, 1,550 soldiers lost their lives.

Racing on the River

Owners cashed in on the speed of their boats. Faster boats meant they could charge higher prices for transporting people and products. Although many owners prohibited their boats from racing, proud captains often couldn't resist the temptation of a river race.

The contest held between the *Natchez* and the *Robert E. Lee* is one of the most famous riverboat races. These competing steamboats usually traveled the 1,200-mile route from New Orleans to St. Louis on alternate days. Thomas Leathers, captain of the *Natchez,* challenged Captain John Cannon of the *Robert E. Lee* to a race. Both men knew the winner would have bragging rights on the Mississippi for years to come.

The race began at about 5:00 p.m. on June 30, 1870. The *Robert E. Lee* immediately took the lead. The speedy *Lee* steamed into St. Louis at 11:25 a.m. on July 4, making the journey in three days, eighteen hours, and fourteen minutes—a new record. The *Natchez* gave the race its best effort but finished more than six hours behind.

Mark Twain, Mississippi Storyteller

Before he became a famous American author, Mark Twain was a Mississippi steamboat pilot. His river tales made the Mississippi popular worldwide. Twain, born Samuel Clemens, grew up in Hannibal, Missouri, a small Mississippi River town. When he decided to pick a unique name for himself as a writer, Samuel Clemens remembered the leadsman calling out the Mississippi's changing depths, "Half twain! Quarter twain! Mark twain!" From then on, Mark Twain and the Mississippi were linked together forever.

In his book *Life on the Mississippi,* Twain said this about a glass of muddy Mississippi water: "Every tumblerful of it holds nearly an acre of land … If you will let your glass stand half an hour, you can separate the land from the water … you will find them both good: the one good to eat, the other good to drink. The land is very nourishing, the water is thoroughly wholesome."

President Lincoln called Vicksburg the "key" to winning the Civil War. After months of siege, the city finally surrendered to General Ulysses S. Grant on July 4, 1863. With Vicksburg's fall, the Mississippi became a Union river.

Mark Twain made his reputation telling Mississippi River tales. Many other folks also had tales to tell about the mighty, misty, muddy, mysterious, maddening, magical, mean, meandering, musical, murky, messy, magnificent, mystical, mythical Mississippi.

OLD AL, KING OF THE MISSISSIPPI, A TALL TALE

Old Al the alligator, king of the Mississippi, enjoyed a fine life on the river. He wore a gold crown, smoked a pipe, and was the biggest, fiercest, orneriest, hungriest gator ever seen. Why, his swishing tail alone created the Mississippi's swirling currents! When Old Al shoveled up sand with his gigantic snout, he made thousands of dangerous sandbars just waiting to catch a steamboat. When he was angry, Old Al plucked people off a boat's deck and flung them into the sticky Mississippi mud. Some folks even say the thick Mississippi fog is just Old Al smoking his pipe.

The Civil War

President Lincoln, who had rafted down the Mississippi as a young man, understood the Mississippi's strategic importance when the Civil War broke out in 1861. Lincoln ordered the Union Army to move down and the Union Navy to move up the Mississippi. Lincoln hoped to split the Confederate states west of the river away from those east of the river and to use the Mississippi as a river road into the heart of the South. The river could carry men, horses, cannons, and supplies to the battlefields.

The South was equally determined to control the Mississippi. It needed the river to transport troops, too, and it needed the river to carry cotton to ships sailing to Europe from New Orleans. With the war raging, cotton was becoming increasingly valuable. Great Britain, with its thousands of weaving looms dependent on Southern cotton, paid high prices for any cotton its factories could get. The Confederacy hoped money from the coveted cotton would enable the states to finance the war. The Union Navy blockaded Southern ports to prevent the cotton from being shipped.

The South's plans failed. In 1862 New Orleans fell to the guns of the U.S. Navy, commanded by David G. Farragut. Farragut hoped to freely steam upstream to meet General Ulysses S. Grant, who was moving south on the Mississippi. One stubborn obstacle blocked their way: Vicksburg, Mississippi.

Vicksburg, the Key to Victory

President Lincoln declared, "Vicksburg is the key. The war can never be brought to a close until that key is in our pocket." Farragut and Grant wished to give President Lincoln that key.

New Orleans today is a major U.S. port. Every year thousands of ships from around the world pass through New Orleans on their way to and from America's heartland. New Orleans is nicknamed The Crescent City for the crescent shape of the course of the Mississippi River as it passes by the city.
Steamboats like the *Delta Queen* give modern tourists a glimpse of what life was like aboard a steamboat. With its paddle wheel churning and its calliope piping, the *Delta Queen* travels up and down the Mississippi and Ohio rivers just as the steamboats did during their heyday in the nineteenth century.

33

Perched high on a bluff overlooking the Mississippi, Vicksburg's cannons kept the North from uniting its forces and controlling the river. In addition to being a Southern military stronghold, Vicksburg was a major port for Rebel supplies. Hogs, corn, cattle, soldiers, and weapons were shipped to Vicksburg, where railroads carried them to Southern armies. Millions of cotton bales were shipped to overseas markets from Vicksburg, too. Confederate president Jefferson Davis, like President Lincoln, knew Vicksburg's value, stating that Vicksburg was "the nailhead that held the South's two halves [west of the Mississippi and east of the Mississippi] together."

Vicksburg Surrenders
The Southern Army as well as civilians valiantly defended Vicksburg. Union attacks were repeatedly turned back. During this time, men, women, and children lived in caves they had dug to escape exploding Union artillery shells. They survived by eating rats and mules when food ran out.

Despite their courage and heroism, the people of Vicksburg finally were defeated. On July 4, 1863, the city surrendered to General Grant. The Union Army watched the surrender in silence, admiring the courage of the people of Vicksburg, who had lost their city but won the hearts of Grant's soldiers.

President Lincoln, now that the Mississippi was under Union control, said, "The Father of Waters again goes unvexed to the sea."

The End of the War, the End of an Era
The Civil War ended a major chapter in the Mississippi's story as a river road. The war brought most passenger and freight shipping to a halt. The Mississippi had become a military battleground and highway. After the end of the war, more railroads bridged the Mississippi. People and cargo heading west on the railroads traveled farther, safer, and more cheaply than by river. Some river traffic returned in the 1860s and 1870s but not at the levels seen before the war began.

Today, long barges carry products to and from the world on the mighty Mississippi. Tourists, looking for a glimpse of the Mississippi's magnificent past, enjoy river rides aboard replica steamboats like the *Delta Queen*. The Mississippi did its duty as a major river road for an expanding nation. The Mississippi continues to shape the United States as products and people travel on its winding waters for profit and pleasure.

And the Missouri has more history stored up in any one of her ten thousand bends than this puny Mississippi creek can boast from her source to the New Orleans delta. I know what I'm talkin' about, because I've seen navigatin' on the Missouri beginnin' with the dugouts the Indians hollowed out of tree trunks right down to those floatin' palaces [steamboats].

—Words of a steamboat man in 1866 from the book
   *Old Man River: The Memories of Captain Louis
   Rosche, Pioneer Steamboatman*

Now the Missouri is about equally unsuited to every kind of river craft: too swift for oars, too deep for poles, too crooked for sails, too shallow for keels, and without permanent banks for a towpath.

—Stanley Vestal, Missouri River historian, 1945

The Missouri

The Missouri, Friend or Foe?

The Indians called the wide, muddy river rolling through their lands *Missouri*. Explorers paddling upstream on the brown water called it "Big Muddy." Others, weary from battling the Missouri's turbulent currents, complained the river was "The Mighty Misery." But whether friend or foe, the Missouri River played a unique role in America's story by opening up much of America west of the Mississippi.

The Missouri Flows and Grows

The Missouri begins as three small, fast, rippling streams high in the Rocky Mountains. At Three Forks, Montana, the three streams braid together to form the Missouri. From Three Forks, the Missouri winds her way east and south through or borders Montana, North Dakota, South Dakota, Iowa, Nebraska, Kansas, and Missouri. Four state capitals stand on the Missouri's banks. The Missouri is where the dense woodlands of the East are separated from the windy plains of the West.

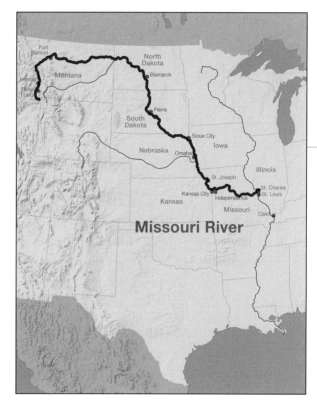

After 2,540 miles, the Missouri mixes her muddy waters with the Mississippi just north of St. Louis. Together, the combined Missouri–Mississippi river system is 3,740 miles long, making it the third-longest river system in the world (after the Nile and the Amazon). Water, falling as snow or rain in the Rocky Mountains, finally finds its way in the Gulf of Mexico and on into the Atlantic.

As the Missouri leaves the mountains and carves through the plains, many tributaries add their waters. The increasingly powerful water cuts into the river's shores, especially during spring floods, and causes the soft-sided banks to cave into the water. As the Missouri moves east, it adds mud to its mix, earning the river the nickname "Muddy Mo'." A Missouri River traveler wrote that the Missouri "is the hungriest river ever created. It is eating all the time—eating yellow clay banks

and cornfields, eighty acres at a mouthful; winding up its banquet with a truck garden and picking its teeth with the timbers of a big red barn."

A UNIQUE RIVER ROAD WEST

The Missouri River stands alone in its role as a river road west. Indians lived along its banks for centuries and still do today. Explorers, trappers, traders, adventurers, pioneers, soldiers, and immigrants traveled up the river's seemingly endless current. Dugout canoes, buffalo-skin bullboats, wooden keelboats, rafts, and steamboats ventured west on the Missouri. Each of their adventures added a chapter to the Missouri's amazing story.

The Missouri before Humans Stood on Its Banks

The Missouri, like so many of America's rivers, was shaped by glaciers during the last Ice Age (twelve to fifteen thousand years ago). As the glaciers bulldozed their path south, they blocked rivers flowing north toward Hudson Bay. These rivers were forced to flow south and east away from the towering face of the glaciers. As the glaciers gradually melted, the earth left behind created much of today's Missouri River drainage.

Before humans discovered the Missouri, it was a wilderness. Groves of cottonwood, oak, elm, and willow lined its banks. Tall and short prairie grasses waved in the never-ending winds. The shrill cries of hawks and eagles, the deep bellows of buffaloes, and the sharp barks of prairie dogs drifted over the river.

Beavers dug homes in the soft Missouri banks and dammed hundreds of streams running into the river. Millions of cranes, white pelicans, ducks, and geese flocked to the Missouri for rest and food. Wolves hunted in the forests and on the open plains. Herds of fleet-footed antelopes darted over the windswept prairies as coyotes chased rabbits and mice. Owls on silent wings hunted at night. Giant grizzlies wandered at will, kings of the Missouri wilderness.

The weather was as varied as the animals and plants. Bitter winter winds blew, sandstorms raged, summer suns burned, thunderstorms rumbled, and tornadoes spun. Stars sparkled and northern lights danced without any human witnesses.

The Indians and the Missouri

The Missouri River world had changed little when Indians first roamed its banks around ten thousand years ago. Small wandering tribes came to the river for food and water. They followed the seemingly endless bison herds over the grasslands. The bison were critical to the Indians' survival.

LEFT TO RIGHT

Snags on the Missouri (an 1841 lithograph from the Karl Bodmer painting). The Missouri was a vital river road in the West. Travelers in canoes as well as steamboats carefully avoided the Missouri's many treacherous sandbars and snags.

Indians lived along the Missouri River from the Mississippi to the Rocky Mountains. Some, like the Mandan, built permanent villages on the banks of the Missouri. Others traveled on and hunted along the river. Here, Indians race their birchbark canoes on the Missouri.

THE BISON, A STORE ON FOUR HOOVES

For many Indians, prehistoric as well as historic, a bison was a store on four hooves. The huge beasts were the Indians' primary source of meat and fat. They scraped the fur off the hides and tanned them with buffalo brains to make soft leather. The Indians fashioned the leather into shirts, skirts, moccasins, quivers, and tipis. Sometimes the thick fur was left on the skins for warm robes and blankets. Bison bones were shaped and sharpened into needles, drills, and awls. Skulls were used in religious practices. The curved horns were carved into cups, ladles, and spoons. Whole horns were used to carry fire or water. Hooves were boiled to make glue. The tough sinews became strings for bows and thread for stitching clothes and tipis.

Around AD 850, some of the Indian bands began settling along the Missouri's banks. They gave up their nomadic lifestyles and built permanent villages, creating great round mounds for homes that were warm in winter and cool in summer. They farmed the fertile soils of the river's bottomlands.

The bountiful Missouri supplied them with fish as well as water for themselves and their gardens. The Indians bathed and swam in the Missouri. Trees by the riverside were a source of wood for fuel, shelter, and shade. Wandering herds of deer, elk, and bison came to the river to drink. Just as their ancestors did, these Indians hunted the animals for meat to eat, bones to shape into tools, and skins for clothes and tipis.

The Missouri became central to the lives of the Blackfeet, Gros Ventre, Shoshone, Mandan, Sioux, Pawnee, Otoes, Arikara, and Omahas. Some of these native peoples continued to roam the open plains, while others settled into living year-round near the Missouri.

The Missouri was an Indian river road as well. Paddling in canoes carved out of logs or bobbing in buffalo-skin bullboats, Indians traveled up, down, and across the wide Missouri. The river was a major link in the widespread Indian trading system. Obsidian for arrow points moved down the river from the Rockies, while shells from the Gulf of Mexico were traded upstream. Copper from the Great Lakes region moved west on the Missouri, and thick buffalo robes were transported east.

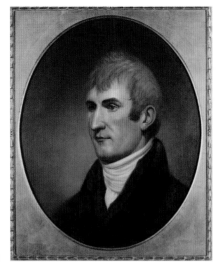

LEFT TO RIGHT
Meriwether Lewis and William Clark

HORSES CHANGE THE PLAINS

The Spanish had brought horses to Mexico in the early 1500s. Some horses escaped and were later captured by the Indians. The Indians bred the horses, which took to life on the grassy plains with ease. Over the next three hundred years, horses gradually spread farther north through trade and raids, transforming the Plains Indians' way of life. No longer did they have to walk long distances to hunt or travel. On horseback they easily followed the roaming bison herds, moving their camps as the bison moved. Horses enabled the Indians to extend their trading ranges, too. The strong animals carried heavy packs loaded with food, stone for tools, and skins.

Marquette Meets the Menacing Missouri

In 1673 the French explorer Father Jacques Marquette and his companion Joliet became the first Europeans to see the Missouri. They encountered the Missouri where it meets the Mississippi north of today's St. Louis.

Arriving during the spring flood, Marquette met the Missouri, which was in an ill-tempered mood. He wrote: "We heard a great rushing and bubbling of waters, and saw small islands of floating trees coming from the mouth of the Pekitanoni (Missouri River) with such rapidity that we could not trust ourselves to go near it. The water of this river is so muddy that we could not drink it." The French explorers refused to venture up the raging river.

The Voyageurs

In the early 1700s, however, hardy French voyageurs were not to be stopped by the the river's fierceness. The voyageurs coveted the plentiful beavers living along the Missouri. Undaunted by the river's powerful currents, dangerous driftwood, and vicious storms, the voyageurs struggled upstream, paddling to the steady rhythm of their songs.

Derrièr' chez nous, y a t'un étang,
Fal ra de la.
Trois beaux canards s'en vont baignant.
Fal ra de la.

"Way back home there is a pond
Fal ra de la.
Three bonnie ducks go swimming on.
Fal ra de la."

Upstream, the voyageurs eagerly traded pots, kettles, knives, pins, needles, guns, and gunpowder to Indian hunters for precious beaver pelts. The voyageurs raced their heavily loaded canoes downstream to enjoy the profits the valuable furs brought them.

Lewis and Clark and the Corps of Discovery

In 1804 Captains Meriwether Lewis and William Clark

This replica of Lewis and Clark's keelboat arrives at Hartford, Illinois, on the Mississippi River, just across from the mouth of the Missouri River.
As the Corps of Discovery neared the Three Forks in Montana, the Missouri grew increasingly shallow. The men often had to walk in the cold water, pulling their heavy dugouts against the strong current.

added experienced Missouri River voyageurs to their expedition. The captains needed the voyageurs' river skills and knowledge to accomplish their waterway journey west across the continent. President Thomas Jefferson, who had dreamed of this expedition for years, hoped that Lewis and Clark would indeed find the Northwest Passage.

Meriwether Lewis and William Clark were already friends from their years in the United States Army when they met at the Falls of the Ohio near Louisville in 1803. They joined forces to finalize their plans for the Corps of Discovery. Lewis had arrived on a large keelboat built in Pittsburgh. Clark had traveled by land.

The expedition's keelboat was loaded with supplies: rifles, gunpowder, knives, lead for bullets, clothes, kettles, axes, chisels, nails, fishing line, spoons, cups, plates, and dozens of other necessary items. The keelboat also carried gifts for Indians: glass beads, cloth, kettles, mirrors, blankets, scissors, colored ribbons, needles, paint, combs, knives, and tomahawks. The keelboat was the corps's store, for they would be months, maybe years, in the wilderness, far from any other place to get supplies.

When they pushed off in their keelboat from the falls, Lewis and Clark began a river journey that changed American history. They floated down the Ohio, poled up the Mississippi, set up winter camp in Illinois, and entered the Missouri River in May 1804.

PRESIDENT JEFFERSON'S ORDERS

President Thomas Jefferson gave Lewis and Clark their orders: "The object of your mission is to explore the Missouri river, & such principal stream of it, as, by it's course & communication with the water of the Pacific ocean may offer the most direct & practicable water communication across the continent, for the purposes of commerce.

"Beginning at the mouth of the Missouri, you will take observations of latitude and longitude at all remarkable points on the river. … Your observations are to be taken with great pains & accuracy."

President Jefferson also instructed Lewis and Clark to establish friendly relations with all Indian tribes they encountered. In addition, they were to record the weather, plants, animals, soil, and minerals they found along the way.

"We Proceeded On"

Clark wrote in his journal on May 14, 1804. "Set out at 4 oClock P.M. … and proceeded on under a jentle brease up the Missourie to the upper Point of the 1st island 4 Miles."

In the keelboat and two pirogues (a type of flat-bottomed boat that can be sailed, rowed, and pulled), the Corps of Discovery struggled upstream with enough food, supplies, and gifts to fill three of today's semitrailers. After years of preparation, the expedition was finally underway.

***York*, a watercolor by Charles M. Russell, 1908.** York, William Clark's African American slave, traveled the entire distance with the expedition. His many skills helped the corps overcome numerous obstacles. Here inside a Mandan earth lodge along the Missouri River, York is examined by Indians who could not believe that the color of his skin did not rub off.

Lewis and Clark spent all summer and fall working their way slowly upstream. Along the way they attempted to establish good relations with the Indians, as President Jefferson had requested. Lewis and Clark, through sign language and translation, told the Indians that now they lived under the government of the United States. Since late 1803, ownership of the Missouri River region had changed from France to the United States with the purchase of Louisiana.

During the long, brutally cold winter, the expedition lived at Fort Mandan. The Americans built their fort near a large Mandan Indian village on the banks of the Missouri in today's North Dakota. In the spring of 1805 Sacagawea (a Shoshone Indian), her baby Pomp, and her husband Charbonneau accompanied the Corps of Discovery at Fort Mandan. As they traveled up the Missouri, Sacagawea shared her native knowledge of plants and animals with Lewis and Clark. Later, when Lewis and Clark needed horses to cross the snowcapped Rocky Mountains, Sacagawea persuaded her brother, Chief Cameahwait, to share Shoshone horses with the Americans.

The Three Forks of the Missouri

In late July 1805, Lewis and Clark reached Three Forks, in southwestern Montana, where three small rivers intertwine to form the headwaters of the Missouri River. In doing so, Lewis and Clark became the first white men to travel the entire length of the Missouri. The explorers wrote in their combined journal: "The S.W. [southwest] fork we called Jefferson's River in honor of that illustrious personage," "the Middle fork we called Maddison's river in honor of James Maddison" and "the S.E. [southeast] fork … we called Gallatin's river in honor of Albert Gallatin Secretary of the Treasury."

After leaving the Missouri, Lewis and Clark crossed the Rockies and voyaged down the Columbia River to the Pacific Ocean. After wintering near the roaring Pacific at Fort Clatsop in Oregon, the expedition headed east toward home in March 1806. That summer, they once again traveled on the Missouri, this time heading downstream.

Lewis and Clark Return

On September 23, 1806, about eight thousand weary miles later, Lewis and Clark finally reached St. Louis. The Missouri River had been their greatest challenge. Mile after twisting mile, the men had battled strong currents, drifting wood, treacherous sandbars, snags as sharp as daggers, and violent winds. They endured blinding sandstorms, pounding hail, ice, numbing temperatures, and scorching heat. An enemy on the upstream trip, the "Mighty Misery" became their friend when returning home. A journey that took almost eleven months struggling upstream against the Missouri's current took less than two months racing downstream.

Lewis and Clark shared the wonders they had seen: beaver, buffalo, elk, deer, bears, and birds without number; Indians eager to trade; plants and animals never before seen by people east of the Mississippi. Much to their disappointment, however, Lewis and Clark proved once and for all that a waterway west across America did not exist. The centuries-old dream of a Northwest Passage crossing the continent ended with the return of Lewis and Clark. Although their tireless efforts proved that there was no Northwest Passage, the information they gathered encouraged thousands of pioneers to venture west on rivers and overland trails.

The Missouri, Nineteenth-Century Expressway

Word of the Missouri's wonders and wealth spread quickly. Adventuresome trappers and traders sought their fortunes up the Missouri. Because of the friendly relations Lewis and Clark had established with most Indian tribes, traders found welcome customers for their goods. Canoes and flatboats loaded with kettles, gunpowder, steel knives and axes, wool blankets, needles, beads, and other trade goods pushed up the Missouri. These same vessels returned to St. Louis brimming with bales of beaver pelts destined for the hatmakers of America and Europe. Fortified trading posts, or "forts," blossomed along the Missouri as the fur trade reached its heyday between 1820 and 1840, especially with the coming of steamboats.

THE FIRST MISSOURI STEAMBOAT

In 1819, the *Independence*, the first Missouri River steamboat, churned upstream. One Missouri newspaper wrote: "We may truly regard this event as highly important, not only to the commercial but agricultural interests of the country. [Through] The practicability of steamboat navigation, being now clearly demonstrated by experiment, we shall be brought nearer to the Atlantic, West Indian, and European markets, and the abundant resources of our fertile and extensive region will be quickly developed."

The Missouri did its best to defeat steamboats. Snags ripped out boat bottoms. The ships' boilers, clogged with gummy Missouri River mud, exploded. Roaring winds prevented passage. Ice crushed fragile wooden hulls. Riverbanks caved in. The river changed channels. Boats ran aground in low water.

But the steamboats succeeded even against the Missouri's currents, winds, sandbars, shallows, and floods. In 1859 there were more steamboats on the Missouri than on the entire Mississippi River! By 1865 steamboats regularly traveled 2,300 miles from St. Louis to Fort Benton, Montana, where the river grew too shallow for them to go any farther.

In 1867 Fort Benton was a major American port, although it was thousands of miles inland from the sea.

Fort Benton, Montana, was the end of the Missouri River road for steamboats. Beyond the fort, the Missouri grew too shallow for them to travel. Tons of supplies for western settlers, soldiers, and miners were unloaded at the fort. Gold and furs were packed onto boats for transport downstream to St. Louis and beyond.

In that year, about forty steamboats, ten thousand passengers, eight thousand tons of mining equipment, and seven thousand tons of food and supplies were unloaded at Fort Benton. From the docks, twenty-five hundred men drove six thousand wagons transporting people and products to the mines, ranches, and farms of the West.

Westward Ho!

Some settlers, like the famous scout Daniel Boone, had already carved out farms in the lands bordering the Missouri. Other settlers followed in his pioneering footsteps. Thousands of eager pioneers, miners, soldiers, and settlers rode high and dry aboard steamboats up the Missouri. For many more folks heading west, however, the Missouri was only the first stage of their journey.

Because they stood on the Missouri's banks, towns like St. Joseph, St. Charles, and Independence became major stopping places for pioneers heading west. The famous Sante Fe, Mormon, Oregon, and California trails branched out from these mushrooming towns. Supplies for the months-long overland wagon trips were easily shipped to the river towns and then sold to pioneers and miners rolling west. Traders also carried their goods along these same trails to distant western markets.

The transcontinental railroad made travel west cheaper, faster, and safer. Over the thirty years that pioneers used the overland trails (roughly 1840–1870), some 350,000 folks moved west in wagons. In 1870, the first year of the transcontinental railroad's operation, trains carried more than 100,000 travelers west.

An Exciting Era Continues

As with so many river roads west, the transcontinental railroad and other railroads brought changes to Missouri's river traffic as hissing steam locomotives replaced chugging steamboats.

The Missouri's importance, however, lasted well into the 1870s. When rich gold and silver mines were discovered in Montana and the Black Hills of South Dakota, steamboats carried the heavy mining equipment to places the railroads didn't reach.

In 1865, after the Civil War ended, the U.S. Army was faced with the challenge of defending American miners and travelers. Indians, fighting to preserve their own western way of life, were a threat to people settling on their lands. Thousands of soldiers and tons of supplies were transported on the Missouri to army forts on the river. Other forts were supplied by goods carried up the Missouri, then hauled by wagons to the soldiers.

Before a bridge crossed the Missouri at Bismarck, Dakota Territory, rails were laid across the frozen river to keep the trains rolling.

THE STEAMBOAT *FAR WEST*

The *Far West* played two key roles in General George Armstrong Custer's final days. In late June 1876, Custer and his generals met aboard the steamboat on the Yellowstone River. The generals made their final plans to attack the Sioux and Cheyenne camped near the Little Big Horn River in Montana. The United States government had ordered the Sioux and Cheyenne to return to their reservations, but the Indians had refused. General Custer planned to attack the Indians, defeat them, and force them back to the reservations.

On June 25 General Custer and his men were surrounded and killed by the Indians. Not one U.S. Army soldier survived. News of General George Custer's defeat at Little Big Horn was carried by the *Far West* down the Missouri to Fort Lincoln, Dakota Territory. From there, word of Custer's Last Stand was telegraphed to a stunned nation, just celebrating America's first one hundred years that July 4.

The Missouri's Heyday Ends

Before the nineteenth century ended, much of the Missouri's wilderness and wildness had disappeared beneath the plow. Where once millions of birds had flocked and buffalo roamed, farms flourished. Cities spread where Indian villages had thrived. Canoes, keelboats, and steamboats were now outpaced by rumbling railroads. Few folks on their way west traveled on the Missouri. Most crossed the Big Muddy on bridges.

Today, dams control a river that once flowed freely. With the dams comes more water for irrigation, turning dry lands into productive farms. Now the river traffic on the Missouri is mostly barges carrying loads of grain from the heartland to the rest of the world.

For many folks, the water behind the dams provides recreational opportunities where most lakes were once little more than ponds. Lewis and Clark battled the Missouri for survival. Today's adventurers on the river relax and enjoy themselves by boat, kayak, and canoe.

But echoes of those days when the muddy, sometimes miserable, but always challenging Missouri was a vibrant river road can still be heard on its waters. They are just harder to hear.

I-o-ho, wonder-water,

I-o-ho, wonder-water,

Life anew to him who drinks!

Look where southwest clouds

   are bringing rain;

Look where southeast clouds

   are bringing rain!

Life anew to him who drinks!

I-o-ho, wonder-water,

I-o-ho, wonder-water,

Life anew to him who drinks!

— Ancient Laguna Indian song
   recorded in New Mexico in the
   early 1900s by Natalie Curtis

Colorado River

The Rio Grande and the Colorado

Two Rivers, Different Destinies

The Colorado River and the Rio Grande begin high in the snow-covered Rocky Mountains in Colorado. Although the two rivers share the same icy origins, their destinies differ.

The Colorado flows west and southwest out of the mountains, carving the Grand Canyon. After twisting and turning for 1,450 miles, the Colorado mixes its freshwater with the salty water of the Gulf of California, a long arm of the Pacific Ocean.

The Rio Grande begins within two hundred miles of the Colorado before winding its way south and southeast for 1,885 miles and trickling into the Gulf of Mexico.

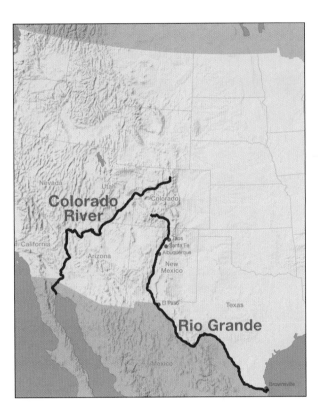

The Colorado and Rio Grande follow different routes to the sea, but their history is woven together. They both flow through some of the most wide open and harsh land in the United States and Mexico. The rivers begin in the mountains, cut through the tallest plateaus, carve the deepest canyons, and cross the widest deserts in North America. As they flow through these arid regions, the rivers bring life. They water the roots of trees, grasses, and shrubs. Animals burrow in the riverbanks and seek shade and food among the plants. Birds dip down for lifesaving sips as they fly their migration routes north and south.

The Continental Divide

What causes the Colorado River to flow west to the Pacific and the Rio Grande to flow east to the Gulf? The answer is the Continental Divide.

The Continental Divide is the line defining the Atlantic and Pacific watersheds. Water that falls as rain or snow on the eastern side of the divide eventually flows into the Gulf of Mexico and on into the Atlantic. Water

LEFT TO RIGHT

As the Rio Grande winds it way down out of the mountains in Colorado, it cuts a deep gorge in New Mexico, which forced explorers and settlers to make long detours.

Indians lived in the Mesa Verde region for centuries. Dozens of families resided in the apartment-like Cliff Palace until about AD 1300 when they mysteriously moved away. This photo of Cliff Palace was taken in the early 1900s.

on the western side of the divide reaches the Pacific. The North American Continental Divide lies high along the backbone of the mountains stretching from Canada to Mexico. In Colorado, the Continental Divide follows the high ridges of the Rockies. Every continent except Antarctica has a continental divide.

The Colorado's Source

The Colorado's headwaters lie in Rocky Mountain National Park. Water from heavy snowfalls, melting glaciers, and falling rain runs off the peaks, gathers in streams, and pools in wetlands before tumbling downhill to form the Colorado. Gathering its first water in the Never Summer mountain range, the Colorado falls more than fourteen thousand feet from its source to its mouth at sea level.

The Colorado adds tributaries to its growing strength on its journey to the sea. Small streams as well as the Green, Gunnison, Dolores, San Juan, Virgin, Little Colorado, and Gila rivers contribute their water to the Colorado. The Colorado passes through parts of Colorado, Utah, Arizona, Nevada, California, and northwestern Mexico. Beginning as a crystal-clear creek in the mountains, the Colorado becomes red with eroded silt and soil. The Spanish explorer Juan de Oñate gave the Colorado its name in 1605 from the Spanish word for the river's reddish color.

The Rio Grande's Source

The Rio Grande, like the Colorado, begins in the Rocky Mountains. Five fast-flowing creeks high in the mountains unite to become the Rio Grande. The early Spanish explorers called the river *El Rio Bravo del Norte,* the Swift River of the North. Later, the river was called the *Rio Grande,* or Big River.

Flowing out of Colorado, the Rio Grande cuts through the center of New Mexico and into Texas. There, the Rio Grande forms the 1,251-mile-long border between Texas and Mexico.

The Anasazi, "The Ancient Ones"

Ten thousand years ago the Southwest was wetter than it is today. The nomadic people living in the region hunted large animals like bison, mammoths, and mountain goats. Rabbits and other small animals also fell prey to their sharp arrows. Pine, juniper, and cottonwood furnished fuel and building materials. Lush plants easily grew in the wet environment. Nuts, roots, and berries were plentiful. These early Indians lived in groups of about forty people each, moving from place to place in search of game and plants.

Over time, however, the rains came less frequently. The Southwest became arid. Hunting and gathering food became more difficult. The native peoples had to find a different way of surviving if they wanted to live in the region. They began farming.

Cliff Palace today.

The Rio Grande, the Colorado, and other, smaller rivers contributed to this new way of life for these ancient inhabitants, often called the Anasazi or "Ancient Ones." Instead of roaming the landscape, around two thousand years ago the Anasazi constructed homes near the life-giving rivers. They used the precious water for drinking, bathing, and growing cotton, corn, beans, and squash.

Some Anasazi grew crops in the rich soils beside the rivers. Others carried water to gardens high atop mesas or laboriously built irrigation systems to bring water to remote fields. Everyone depended on the rivers, streams, or springs for survival.

Mesa Verde, in southwestern Colorado, is one of the most famous of these ancient places. People lived in the Mesa Verde area for more than seven hundred years, from about AD 600 until about AD 1300. Early Anasazi built round underground homes near their gardens. Later Mesa Verde inhabitants built more elaborate cliff dwellings out of stone and adobe. Several of these apartment-like buildings were five stories tall.

Around AD 1300, the ancient people abandoned their homes and fields. Archaeologists are trying to discover whether dry weather, depleted soil, or human enemies caused the people to leave their homes. The Ancient Ones moved out of the cliff dwellings but not away from the region. Today, twenty-four Indian tribes living in the Southwest have ancestors who once lived in the Mesa Verde area.

After AD 1300, many Indians built villages on flat-topped mesas. Their towns, which the Spanish called pueblos, were made of stone and adobe. These builders made paint by crushing local rocks, which added a yellow color to their dwellings. When the Spanish learned about these yellow-walled cities, they assumed the buildings were made of gold. Eager for easy wealth, the Spanish set out to find these cities of gold, the fabled Seven Cities of Cíbola. The coming of the Spanish in the 1500s influenced the history of the Colorado River and the Rio Grande.

THE MYTH OF THE GOLDEN KING OF EL DORADO

The Golden King of El Dorado particularly intrigued the Spanish. Every morning this mighty Indian king was washed in oil. Tiny flecks of gold were sprinkled over his body, clinging to the oil and covering the king from head to toe. The king remained as golden as the sun. In the evening the Golden King washed off his gold in a lake. Over the centuries the lake's bottom became covered with gold, gold that the Spanish coveted.

The Cities of Gold

Soon after Columbus crossed the Atlantic in 1492, Spanish adventurers went to the Americas searching for gold. From the Indians they heard stories of the Seven Cities of Cíbola whose streets were paved with gold and whose

Coronado's March, after the illustration by Frederic Remington in 1898. Spaniard Francisco de Coronado and his army marched through the Southwest looking for the Seven Cities of Cíbola. Their wanderings took them from Mexico north into present-day Kansas. They never found the fabled cities, but they did stumble upon the Grand Canyon.

golden walls glittered. These Seven Cities were said to be somewhere in the Southwest. The Spanish hoped to use the Rio Grande and the Colorado River as routes to guide them to the wonderful wealth of the fabled Seven Cities.

But the Spanish were disappointed. Unlike many other American rivers, the Colorado and Rio Grande proved difficult as river roads. They ran too fast in the spring with rushing meltwater. In summer, the rivers slowed to a trickle in the searing heat. They were too rocky, too shallow, and too hard to reach for easy travel into the interior of the Southwest.

Coronado's Quest

By the early 1500s, the Spanish conquistadors (conquerors) controlled much of Mexico. From Mexico City, their capital, they sent expeditions to the lands of the North. Gold was their goal.

In 1540 the Mexican viceroy Antonio de Mendoza, greedy for gold, ordered an expedition led by Francisco de Coronado to find the Seven Cities of Cíbola.

Coronado set out with 336 soldiers, 5 priests, and 800 Mexicans and their families. Thousands of pigs, sheep, goats, and cattle trailing behind provided fresh meat for the expedition. By midsummer the army reached Hawikuh, the first of the fabled Seven Cities. After a fierce battle with Hawikuh's inhabitants, Coronado quickly realized the town was an adobe pueblo, not a city of gold.

Coronado was determined to find the remaining six cities of Cíbola. Instead of marching all his men to one place and then another, Coronado sent scouts to find the cities. Coronado chose Captain García de Cárdenas to march northwest.

After many days crossing the burning desert lands, Cárdenas found his way blocked by an immense canyon. Gazing a mile down, Cárdenas saw the tiny thread of a river winding its way far below the cliff tops. Cárdenas and his men became the first Europeans to see the Colorado River and to peer into the canyon that would one day be called the Grand Canyon. Staring into its depths, Cárdenas saw there was no way across the abyss, so he turned back.

Captain Cárdenas told Coronado the disappointing news that a canyon prevented any further exploration to the northwest. He also told him there were no golden cities in that direction either.

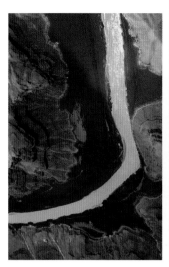

The Grand Canyon was carved by the Colorado River over millions of years. As the churning river slices down into the earth, multicolored layers of rocks are revealed. From its deepest point, the Grand Canyon rises more than one mile to its rim. Despite the canyon's great depth, Indians lived and farmed along the Colorado River for centuries. However, the Grand Canyon was a major obstacle to the exploration of the West.

THE GRAND CANYON

The Grand Canyon is one of America's best-known natural wonders. The powerful, persistent Colorado River has cut through thick layers of rock hundreds of feet thick to carve the canyon. Nature has taken forty million years to shape the canyon as it winds its way for 277 miles through the northwestern corner of Arizona. One tall tale, however, has the legendary logger Paul Bunyan creating the Grand Canyon as he drags his huge, heavy ax behind him while walking through the region.

After Cárdenas in 1540, Father Francisco Garcés was the next European to see the Grand Canyon. He stood on the canyon's edge in 1776. Today, millions of visitors from around the world enjoy the wonders of the Grand Canyon. Many stand on the canyon's rim looking down into the depths. More adventuresome tourists ride rafts and wooden boats on the Colorado, seeing the canyon from the bottom up. For geologists, who study the earth's history, the Grand Canyon is like a window into the past, revealing more than a billion years of rock formation and erosion.

Settlers Come to the Southwest

Through letters and journals, the Spanish spread the word about the people they had met and the places they had explored. Their accounts lured others to the lands of the Southwest. Catholic priests from Mexico and Spain went into the wilderness to convert the Indians to Christianity. Settlers pioneered homes. Traders crisscrossed the mountains and wide-open places bartering with the Indians and Spanish. Sante Fe, New Mexico, near the Rio Grande, became the most important city of Spanish America. From Sante Fe, Spanish influence spread throughout the Southwest over the next two hundred years.

By the 1800s the residents of the young United States to the east had heard about the climate, land, and business opportunities of the Southwest centered on the Rio Grande. More and more Americans began to settle in the region. Many used the Rio Grande as their guidepost.

Beaver, the Real Gold

The western mountains proved to have treasure after all. The wealth was not gold or jewels but beavers. Beaver pelts were used primarily to make hats that were extremely popular with Europeans. As the supply of beavers had dwindled in the East, trappers discovered the beavers living in the wetlands and rivers of the West. Millions of beavers that swam in the waters feeding the Colorado and the Rio Grande were easy pickings for hardy hunters.

Major John Wesley Powell explored the Grand Canyon in 1869 and 1871. These photographs were taken during his second expedition. Left: Leaving from Green River City, Wyoming. Right: For both expeditions, Powell named his boat the *Emma Dean*, in honor of his wife. Powell rode in a chair atop his boat so he could see what dangers lay ahead and to guide the expeditions.

Trappers, like those of the Missouri River region, used beaver pelts to trade for the traps, guns, knives, blankets, pans, salt, and lead bullets they needed to carry out their business. The trappers ranged over the West looking for new streams with plenty of beavers.

Two major trading posts grew in the region to supply the trappers and settlers. Bent's Fort on the Arkansas River served people on the eastern slope of the Rockies. Taos, near the Rio Grande, served those on the southwestern slope. For many years a moving gathering, or "rendezvous," met the needs of the trappers in the Colorado River basin.

Most trappers were from the United States. As they moved into the Southwest, the Mexicans governing the region grew increasingly displeased. The Mexicans didn't want to be outnumbered by the Americans who might end up taking their lands.

Tensions between Mexico and the United States reached a head when Texas declared its independence in 1836. For the next nine years Texas was an independent nation with the Rio Grande as its southern border with Mexico. In 1845 Texas joined the United States as the twenty-eighth state in the Union.

The next year—1846—Mexico and the United States went to war. Soldiers and citizens from both countries died as Mexico tried to save its lands and the United States fought to take them. Robert E. Lee and Ulysses S. Grant, two future generals who would fight against each other in the Civil War, served together in the Mexican-American War.

One of the favorite songs soldiers sang to their sweethearts before heading off to the war was "Way, You Rio."

Oh, say, were you ever in the Rio Grande?
Way, you Rio.
It's there that the river runs down to golden sand.
For we're bound to the Rio Grande.
And away, you Rio!
Way, you Rio!
Sing fare you well
My pretty young girls,
For we're bound to the Rio Grande!

When the war ended in 1848, Mexico had lost its lands north of the Rio Grande and west to California. The United States now stretched from sea to shining sea.

Hoover Dam is east of Las Vegas, Nevada. The towering dam holds back the Colorado River so its waters can be used to generate electricity and provide water for the farms and cities of the arid Southwest.

Filling in the Last Blank Spot on America's Map

Slowly, the map of the western United States was being filled in. By the end of the Civil War in 1865, the largest unmapped space was in the heart of the West. This empty region was called the Great Unknown. Today we know it as the Grand Canyon. In all the years of exploring and trapping, no one had gone down the Colorado River through the Grand Canyon and lived to tell the tale. Knowledgeable Indians warned that the rushing waters would kill anyone who tried.

Major John Wesley Powell became determined to fill in this last empty place on the map of America. Powell had lost an arm in the Civil War, but he hadn't lost his courage. In May 1869, with nine companions, Major Powell set off in four wooden boats. After months of hardship and hunger, Powell, five men, and two boats emerged from the depths of the Grand Canyon on August 29, 1869. The men had been given up for lost. But with extreme courage they surprisingly survived to reveal the last secrets of the Colorado River. The Colorado was now explored from its headwaters in Colorado to its mouth in Mexico.

Major Powell wrote: "We had emerged from the Grand Canyon of the Colorado! The relief from danger and the joy of success were great. Ever before us had been the unknown. Nearly every waking hour passed in the Grand Canyon had been one of toil, hardship, and hunger.

… But now the danger was over, the toil had ceased, the gloom disappeared. The river rolled by us in silent majesty. The quiet of camp was sweet after the incessant roar of the river. Our joy was almost ecstasy."

After Powell's explorations (also in 1871), the Colorado River and the Rio Grande were mapped. They had never been easy river highways into the West. But over the centuries the two rivers were obstacles, then landmarks for those who explored, settled, and populated the region. The Colorado and the Rio Grande still supply life-giving water from Texas to California as well as exceptional outdoor adventures for today's explorers.

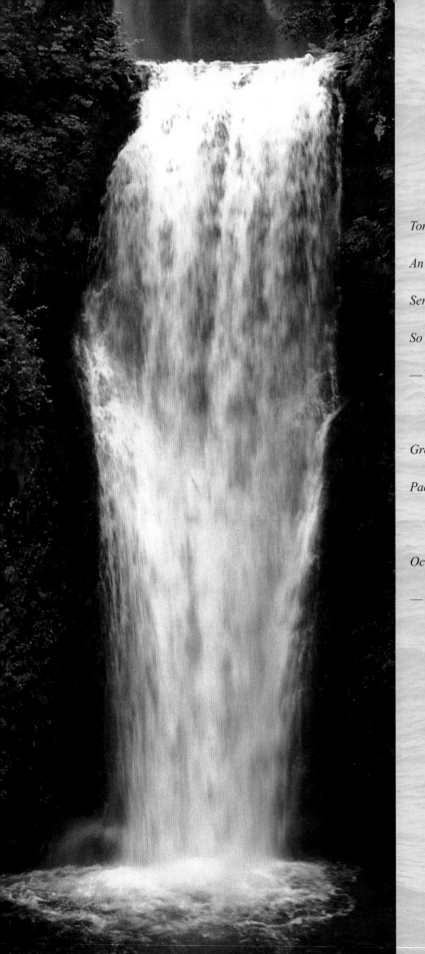

Tom Jefferson's vision would not let him rest

An empire he saw in the Pacific Northwest

Sent Lewis and Clark and they did the rest

So roll on, Columbia, roll on

—Woody Guthrie, twentieth-century
   American songwriter

Great joy in camp we are in View of the Ocian, this great

Pacific Octean which we been So long anxious to See.

~

Ocian in view! O! the joy.

—Captain William Clark, Corps of Discovery, 1805

The Columbia

The Great River of the West

The Columbia is called "The Great River of the West" and with good reason. Flowing out of the Rocky Mountains to the Pacific Ocean, the Columbia is the largest river of the West Coast of the United States.

Columbia Lake, high in the mountains of British Columbia, Canada, is the headwaters for the Columbia River. Snow and rain from two mountain ranges fill Columbia Lake: the Purcell peaks to the west and Rockies to the east. Cradled between these mountain ranges, Columbia Lake is cool and clear in the summer and ice-covered in the long winter. Father Pierre De Smet, a Catholic priest, wrote in 1845: "Those rugged and gigantic mountains where the Great River escapes—majestic, but impetuous … and in its vagrant course it is undoubtedly the dangerous river on the western side of the American hemisphere." Father De Smet was correct on both counts; the Columbia was majestic and dangerous.

Spilling out of the lake in a wide, shallow channel, the Columbia River flows 1,232 miles from its source to the ocean. Dozens of rivers and streams, large and small, add their waters to the Columbia as it journeys to the Pacific.

The Columbia eventually reaches the Pacific Ocean to the west, but first it runs two hundred miles north. After meandering toward the Arctic, the Columbia flows south at Big Bend. The river continues south, west, then south again before making its final westward turn toward the sea. On this final leg the Columbia forms part of the border between Washington State and Oregon.

The Columbia passes through icy mountains, burning deserts, deep gorges, and lush forests on its determined course to the Pacific. In addition to water from its source in British Columbia, the river is fed by water from Washington, Oregon, Idaho, Montana, Wyoming, Utah, and Nevada.

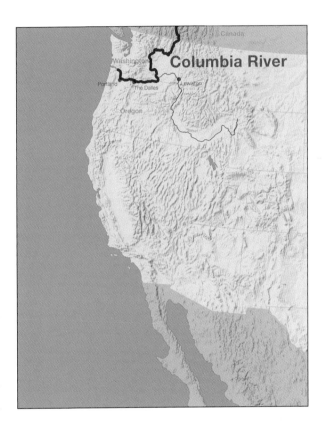

Crown Point, east of Portland, Oregon, overlooks the wide Columbia River. After cascading down out of the mountains, the Columbia broadens as it approaches the Pacific Ocean.

Instead of flowing quietly into the sea in a gentle delta as the Mississippi does, the Columbia creates a treacherous, shifting sandbar at its mouth. From its headwaters to its end, the Columbia is truly the Great River of the West.

The Indians of the Columbia Basin

For many Northwest Indians, the Columbia River region was home. More than thirty different tribes thrived along the banks of the Columbia. The earliest tribes settled at The Dalles on the Columbia around eleven thousand years ago. At The Dalles, the Columbia is squeezed into a narrow channel filled with rapids, falls, and swirling eddies. Because the river is pinched there, millions of salmon migrating upstream every year were forced into a small space where they could be easily speared, caught in nets, or trapped in weirs.

SALMON

Salmon was the key to life for the Indians living along the Columbia River. This is because of the salmon's predictable life. Hatched high in the Columbia's headwaters and tributaries, the tiny salmon swim downstream to the Pacific Ocean. There they live most of their lives feeding and fattening up on plentiful ocean food. When it's time to mate and lay eggs, the determined salmon swim upstream against the Columbia's mighty current, sometimes leaping ten feet up and over waterfalls. The salmon search for the place of their birth, for that is where the females lay their eggs, renewing the salmon cycle.

Each summer and fall the Indians gathered along the rivers during the annual salmon runs. They feasted on the fish, drying some of it for food in the winter. The salmon was the mainstay of life for many Northwest Indians.

The Indians of the Columbia Plateau

Many Indians lived east of the Cascade Mountains, which run north-south in Oregon. Capped with white-tipped volcanoes like Mount Hood and Mount St. Helens, the Cascades keep the coast wetter than the arid, interior plateau country. The Indians living in the plateau region led quite different lives from those along the Pacific Coast. All, however, were dependent on the multitudes of salmon, sturgeon, and trout flourishing in the Columbia and its tributaries.

The Indians east of the Cascades made their homes in the dry, high plateau and in the Rocky Mountains. Theirs was a life shaped by the four seasons. They built circular lodges to weather the bitter winters. Their summer homes were constructed of bulrush mats covering cottonwood frames. They hunted deer, elk, rabbits, and mountain sheep. To supplement their diets, they

Indians living along the Columbia often used dugout canoes for salmon fishing and transportation. In many places the Columbia is a rushing, tumbling river, but it frequently has calm stretches where travel is easy.

Salmon and whitefish were important food sources for the Indians living along the Columbia. They ate the fish fresh and also dried the meat to eat later or to trade. The abundant fish were usually speared or netted either from shore or canoes.

55

gathered nuts and berries. They dug wild onions, carrots, bitterroot, and camas bulbs. Boiled, roasted, or raw camas bulbs were a staple of their diets.

Wood for fires and homes came from the forests. Massive tree trunks were hollowed into long dugout canoes. These dugouts, while heavy, survived the hazards of the rugged rocky rivers much better than fragile birch-bark canoes could.

Like so many rivers, the Columbia was a river road for the Indians. On it the native peoples journeyed throughout the region. After Europeans reached the coast in 1775, glass beads, cloth, nails, steel knives, and guns were bartered among the Indians alongside the more traditional trade goods. Coastal Indians paddled 150 miles upstream to The Dalles (the narrow canyon on the Columbia) to trade with tribes coming from the interior. The tribes from the coast traded sea otter pelts and decorated seashells for deerskins, baskets, and edible roots. The trading tribes portaged around the Columbia's many rapids and falls. In 1805, when Lewis and Clark reached The Dalles, they were surprised to find Indians who had never seen white men trading European products.

The Indians of the Coast

The Coastal Indians could find all they needed from the area surrounding them—the sea and the forests. The coast was frequently windy and wet, but the temperature was mild year-round, with little snow in winter. The moist climate was ideal for the growth of the lush forests that shaped the coastal cultures. The coastal region was so bountiful that these tribes needed little agriculture to sustain them.

From the sea came salmon, cod, trout, herring, and halibut. The abundant, oily eulachon fish was a source of food and light (the eulachon burned like a candle when dried) as well as an important trade item to Indians living inland. Sea otters, seals, sea lions, and whales were hunted for meat or fur. Clams, mussels, and sea urchins were easily gathered at the seashore when the tide was out.

The heavily wooded mountains and hills along the Northwest Coast were the source of wood for homes, sea-going canoes, and fuel. The red and yellow cedar woods were soft and could be worked with stone tools. The Indians used the cedar to make wooden racks to dry fish as well as waterproof boxes and baskets. They split planks from logs to build their snug, dry longhouses. Each long-house was home to many families, sometimes housing more than one hundred people.

Cedars and redwoods were the woods of choice for making dugout canoes. A skilled canoemaker took

Sir Francis Drake was one of England's most famous explorers. Drake's ship the *Golden Hind* landed on the western coast of North America, missing the chance to become the first European to see the Columbia River.

many months cutting, hollowing, shaping, and decorating his canoe. When the dugout was finished, he used it for fishing, hunting, traveling, and trading. Some dugouts held up to fifty people and could be used on the Columbia as well as on the open ocean.

With the coming of the Europeans and their metal tools in the mid-1700s, working with wood became much easier for coastal tribes. The arrival of the Europeans on the West Coast brought many others changes, too.

The Spanish Almost Discover the Columbia River

For years the wide blockade of sand and rocks at the Columbia's mouth hid the river from the prying eyes of explorers.

Many Europeans predicted that there had to be a western river that ran into the sea just as the Hudson and Mississippi did. They hoped this western sea was the other end of the Northwest Passage.

In the 1540s the Spanish came close to finding the Columbia's mouth. Sailing north from their home base in Mexico, the Spanish slowly explored the Pacific Coast. They noted the open grasslands, towering forests, and Indians. The Spanish, hungry for gold and not finding any, left most of the land beyond the coastline unexplored. Little did they know they had bypassed the California gold fields, the richest on earth. Three hundred years would pass before thousands of folks would stampede to California during the gold rush.

The Spanish, with outposts already stretching from Mexico down the western coast of South America, believed the entire Pacific Ocean belonged to them. The Spanish were so sure of themselves that they did little to defend their North American coastal claims.

The English Sail into the Pacific

The English, eager for a share of the wealth of the New World, decided to test the Pacific waters. In 1577 Francis Drake sailed from England. His mission was to sneak into the Pacific, raid Spanish towns, steal their wealth, and search for the Northwest Passage.

Drake did not find the Northwest Passage, but he successfully raided the Spanish. By 1579 his ship was so loaded with Spanish gold and jewels that it couldn't hold any more treasure. So Drake turned to exploring the western coast. Before heading home, he sailed north to where the border is today between the United States and Canada. Along the way he, too, passed the hidden mouth of the Columbia.

The *Columbia* on the Columbia

By the mid-1700s many sea captains knew a great river was somewhere along the Northwest Coast. The Indians had told them about this river. Some had seen evidence of the river entering the ocean. In 1775 Don Bruno de Heceta of Spain noticed a large muddy stain on the ocean, a dirty

President Thomas Jefferson requested that both Lewis and Clark keep journals about their explorations and carefully record the people, places, plants, and animals they saw. William Clark drew this picture of an eulachon, a smelt.

patch that meant fresh inland water was flooding into the sea. Captain James Cook, a British explorer, almost discovered the Columbia, too, in 1778 as he explored the West Coast. The Russians, too, had bypassed the Columbia on their way to hunt sea otter in California.

The honor for the discovery of the Columbia fell to Captain Robert Gray from Boston, an event which placed the Columbia in American hands rather than British. On May 11, 1792, Captain Gray crossed the sandbar at the Columbia's mouth (Gray was lucky—it was an unusually calm day!) and anchored six miles upstream.

To honor his achievement, Captain Gray named the river in honor of his ship, the *Columbia.* Captain Gray carried with him a letter signed by President George Washington. President Washington requested those who met Captain Gray to treat him and his men with kindness and courtesy.

Captain Gray, while not meeting any emperors or kings, was pleased to meet the Indians living along the Columbia. For a week Gray traded with local tribes, giving nails, cloth, and copper for priceless furs. After eight days he had 150 prime otter skins, 300 beaver pelts, and more than 600 skins from other animals.

Worried that he might get trapped behind the Columbia's shifting sandbar, Gray sailed out of the Columbia and back into the Pacific. Captain Gray's short visit established an American claim to the Columbia River region, and just in time. Later that year, Lieutenant William Broughton, an Englishman, entered the Columbia and sailed one hundred miles upstream. Lieutenant Broughton named a snowcapped mountain, the tallest mountain in Oregon, Mount Hood in honor of an English nobleman and naval officer.

News about the discovery of the Columbia's mouth spread quickly. During the next thirteen years, more than one hundred ships sailed into the Columbia to replenish supplies and trade for valuable furs.

Lewis and Clark Finally See the Sea

In 1805 the Americans reestablished their claim to the Columbia. After a year and a half of travel, Lewis and Clark reached the Columbia River on October 16, 1805. In their handmade canoes Lewis and Clark ran the river's many rapids, pausing to portage only a few times. Almost every day the corps encountered Indians with whom they traded for fish and other supplies. Lewis and Clark didn't linger, however, for they were eager to reach the Pacific.

The expedition was exposed to the Columbia's many moods. They battled strong winds. They suffered days and nights of pelting rain. Extremely high tides flooded their campsites. Their clothes rotted from the endless moisture. The crashing waves at the river's mouth challenged them for days. Finally, the Lewis and Clark expedition paddled into the Pacific.

Astoria was established at the mouth of the Columbia River by John Jacob Astor's American Fur Company in 1811. Astor's company and others like it used their settlements to supply the fur trappers of the Northwest. Millions of dollars worth of beaver, elk, mink, and other furs were carried to Astoria and shipped to China, the United States, and Europe.

Lewis and Clark built a log fort and spent the winter before heading home. They chose a protected place on a river emptying into the bay inside the mouth of the Columbia. They named their home Fort Clatsop in honor of the local Indian tribe. There they spent a long, wet, miserable winter before paddling back up the Columbia.

Lewis and Clark left Fort Clatsop on March 23, 1806, and reached St. Louis in September. Their explorations strengthened America's Columbia River claims. Their explorations also proved once and for all that no river road west cut across America. The Northwest Passage had been only a dream after all.

A Tug of War for Oregon

Between 1792 and 1848 the Columbia region was known as the Oregon Territory. The word "Oregon" came from the Plains Indian word *Ouragan,* which French explorers interpreted to mean "The Great River of the West."

Both Americans and British established trading posts in Oregon. These trading posts provided goods and supplies for the trappers and traders who roamed the mountains and the shores seeking furs. These adventurers trapped their own furs or traded with the Indians.

Furs, especially sea otter and beaver, were treasured by the Chinese, who paid high prices for good pelts. Millions of dollars' worth of furs crossed the Pacific to supply eager Chinese buyers. Over time the fur trade dwindled when silk became more popular for hats and beaver grew scarce.

The population of America, however, was rapidly growing. Word spread about the rich farmlands in the Oregon Territory, especially the Willamette Valley south of the Columbia. A few pioneers settled in the valley and sent word home about the free land and the wonderful climate. By the 1840s, hundreds and then thousands of pioneers came to Oregon. Some sailed around South America and up the coast, a journey that took six months. Many more packed their belongings into wagons and rumbled across the continent on the Oregon Trail. The Oregon Trail, although it also took about six months to travel, became the major road west for many Americans.

Many of those traveling along the Oregon Trail used the rivers, too. Folks floated down the Ohio and poled up the Missouri to Independence, St. Joseph, and Westport. There, they hitched oxen to their wagons for the long, dangerous journey across the country. Some split off to head to California, especially when the gold rush began there in the late 1840s. Others, exclaiming "Oregon or Bust," traveled the last hard miles along the Columbia's southern shore where the rushing river had cut a pass through the Cascade Mountains.

 LEFT TO RIGHT
The Columbia River flowed wild and free for a long time. But as the population of the Northwest grew, there was a need to tame the river so steamboats could travel on it. Locks were built around many rapids so that boats could bypass them.

The Grand Coulee Dam in Washington State holds back the Columbia River, creating the 150-mile-long Lake Roosevelt. The dam is the largest concrete structure in the United States. Water flowing over the dam is used to irrigate hundreds of thousands of acres of land. The water is also used to run turbines, which generate electricity for the people of the Northwest.

Great Britain and the United States almost went to war over the Oregon Territory. But so many American settlers had moved to the territory (which included Washington State as well) that the British and the United States settled on an international border rather than fight a war. This border extended from the Great Lakes west to the Pacific along the forty-ninth parallel of latitude.

Steamboats on the Columbia

Steamboats played a role in the Columbia's story. Although the river was hard to navigate in some places, its open stretches made smooth steaming for the boats. The *Beaver* was the first steamboat on the Columbia in 1836. The *Beaver* ran briefly on the lower Columbia near the river's mouth before seeking the safer waters of Puget Sound to the north.

When gold was discovered near Lewiston, Idaho, in the early 1860s, steamboats began regular runs up the river. But these runs were quite short. When the boat met an obstacle, such as the fifteen-mile stretch of rapids at The Dalles, its path was blocked.

To solve this problem, steamboat owners built railroads around the rapids. Cargo and passengers would steam up the Columbia, unload everything onto a train, ride the rails around the rapids, and load everything and everyone onto another steamboat. Fourteen portages were needed between Portland and Lewiston, a time-con-suming and expensive process. Products shipped from the region's interior farms followed the same procedure in reverse to go downstream.

Railroads Bring Changes

In the 1880s the transcontinental railroad and its branch lines brought over five hundred thousand Americans to settle in the Northwest. One of the major routes was down both sides of the Columbia. The river's long, gentle run to the sea and the passage it had cut through the mountains provided an ideal slope for railroad construction. By filling in wetlands and building bridges, railroad engineers were able to lay the tracks easily and quickly. So, instead of one railroad running down a single shore, railroads were built on both banks!

And, as on so many American rivers, the coming of the trains meant the end of the steamboats.

The Columbia's Power

Boats and barges travel the Columbia today using a system of locks and dams. The fourteen dams on the main river and the dams on its tributaries provide three major benefits for the Columbia region. One dam, the Grand Coulee, is the largest concrete structure in the United States. In 1941 Woody Guthrie wrote a song celebrating the dam:

Cast your eyes upon the biggest thing yet built
   by human hands,
On the King Columbia River, it's the big
   Grand Coulee Dam.

The water behind the dams is a key source for irrigation. With Columbia water, farmers have turned arid lands into producing farms. Wheat and fruit grow well in the long, hot inland summers. Today's trucks, trains, ships, and planes carry these products to markets worldwide.

The water stored behind the dams also creates immense amounts of electricity. As the water is released, it spins massive turbines, generating electricity. The Columbia's electricity powers much of the Northwest.

The dams also play a major role in controlling flooding on the Columbia. Every year floods had rolled down the river, destroying the fields, farms, and buildings on the Columbia's banks. Dams hold back the floodwaters, so the water can be released when needed for electricity and irrigation. The dams, however, also prevent the Columbia from flowing freely and flushing itself clean of sediment and debris, much of which is filling in the riverbed behind the dams. And the dams also impact the annual salmon migration. Salmon ladders have been built at some dams to help the salmon climb toward their spawning grounds. A wild river that once rolled freely to the sea has been tamed by man-made dams.

The Columbia, Still the Great River of the West

The Great River of the West was one of the last major rivers discovered and explored by Europeans and white Americans. The Columbia proved to be more of an obstacle than a river road. Much of the Columbia, though tamed by dams today, was a wild, turbulent, rapids-filled river when the first European explorers stumbled upon it and the Indians inhabited its shores. The Columbia plunged out of the mountains, tumbled down waterfalls, rushed through canyons, and carved countless coulees.

The Columbia rolled into history as a destination for Americans seeking a better life. Today, the Columbia works hard furnishing water, electricity, transportation, and recreation for millions of people living and visiting in the Northwest. The turbulent, twisting Columbia was a key to the settling of the Northwest and still plays a vital role in the region's quality of life.

Afterword

For many years the search for the Northwest Passage across the wide North American continent motivated explorers, traders, trappers, and mappers to find a fast path from east to west. After centuries of searching, no waterway west was found. For many people the rivers were their roads for the settlement and development of America.

When the rolling ribbons of steel railroads criss-crossed the country, rivers lost much of their importance as highways for people. Still, every year, millions of tons of cargo move on America's river roads to markets around the world. And many people use the rivers for water and recreation.

Our rivers still roll along. Today, the shrill whistle of a steamboat is heard by tourists enjoying a river adventure on a steamboat replica. Daring travelers venture down the Grand Canyon on rafts or wooden boats. Others visit Indian sites near rivers to get a sense of a time long ago and today. The stories, songs, and tall tales of America's river roads continue to echo. Following our river roads takes us on a journey through America's history.

Further Reading

Books

Cohn, Amy. *From Sea to Shining Sea: A Treasury of American Folklore and Folk Songs.* New York: Scholastic, 1993.

Doherty, Kieran. *Voyageurs, Lumberjacks, and Farmers: Pioneers of the Midwest.* Minneapolis: Oliver Press, 2004.

Emsden, Katharine. *Voices from the West: Life along the Trail.* Lowell, MA: Discovery Enterprises, 1992.

Fraser, Mary Ann. *In Search of the Grand Canyon.* New York: Henry Holt, 1995.

Fraser, Mary Ann. *Vicksburg: The Battle That Won the Civil War.* New York: Henry Holt, 1999.

Graymont, Barbara. *The Iroquois.* New York: Chelsea House, 1988.

Harness, Cheryl. *Mark Twain and the Queens of the Mississippi.* New York: Simon & Schuster, 1998.

Longfellow, H. W. *The Song of Hiawatha.* New York: Dutton & Co., 1963.

Lourie, Peter. *Rio Grande: From the Rocky Mountains to the Gulf of Mexico.* Honesdale, PA: Boyds Mills Press, 1999.

Marrin, Albert. *Empires Lost and Won: The Spanish Heritage in the Southwest.* New York: Atheneum, 1997.

Phelan, Mary Kay. *Waterway West: The Story of the Erie Canal.* New York: Crowell & Co., 1977.

Rawlins, Carol B. *The Colorado River.* New York: Grolier, 1999.

Roop, Peter, and Connie Roop, eds. *The Diary of John Wesley Powell: Conquering the Grand Canyon.* Tarrytown, NY: Marshall Cavendish, 2001.

Roop, Peter, and Connie Roop. *The Louisiana Purchase.* New York: Aladdin, 2004.

Twain, Mark. *Life on the Mississippi.* Mineola, NY: Dover, 2000.

Web Sites* and Places to Visit

Discovering Lewis & Clark. *www.lewis-clark.org*
Thorough Web site dedicated to Lewis and Clark and the Corps of Discovery.

The Erie Canal. *www.eriecanal.org*
Web site with background information on the Erie Canal as well as outstanding images.

Grand Canyon National Park. *nps.gov/grca*
The official Web site of Grand Canyon National Park.

Jefferson National Expansion Memorial. *www.nps.gov/jeff*
Information about the Gateway Arch in St. Louis, Lewis and Clark, and the growth of America.

Lewis & Clark State Historic Site, Wood River, Illinois. *www.campdubois.com*
Replica of site where the expedition spent a winter preparing for the trip up the Missouri. Outstanding displays and activities.

Mark Twain, Boyhood Home & Museum, Hannibal, Missouri. *www.marktwainmuseum.org*
Web site with information for students and teachers about Mark Twain and his life on the Mississippi. Excellent links to other sites about Twain.

Mesa Verde National Park. *nps.gov/meve*
The official Web site of Mesa Verde National Park.

National Mississippi River Museum & Aquarium. *www.mississippirivermuseum.com*
New museum and aquarium with many hands-on, interactive exhibits and numerous Mississippi River aquatic environment aquariums.

* Active at the time of publication

Selected Bibliography

Andrist, Ralph. *Steamboats on the Mississippi.* New York: American Heritage Publishing, 1962.

Baldwin, Leland D. *The Keelboat Age on Western Waters.* Pittsburgh: University of Pittsburgh Press, 1980.

Banta, R. E. *The Ohio.* New York: Rinehart, 1949.

Bernstein, Peter L. *Wedding of the Waters: The Erie Canal and the Making of a Great Nation.* New York: Norton & Co., 2005.

Carmer, Carl Lamson. *The Hudson.* New York: Grosset & Dunlap, 1968.

Cohn, Amy. *From Sea to Shining Sea: A Treasury of American Folklore and Folk Songs.* New York: Scholastic, 1993.

Dietrich, William. *Northwest Passage: The Great Columbia River.* New York: Simon & Schuster, 1995.

Dohan, Mary Helen. *Mr. Roosevelt's Steamboat.* New York: Dodd, Mead, 1981.

Doherty, Kieran. *Voyageurs, Lumberjacks, and Farmers: Pioneers of the Midwest.* Minneapolis: Oliver Press, 2004.

Dolnick, Edward. *Down the Great Unknown.* New York: Harper, 2002.

Emsden, Katharine. *Voices from the West: Life along the Trail.* Lowell, MA: Discovery Enterprises, 1992.

Fraser, Mary Ann. *In Search of the Grand Canyon.* New York: Henry Holt, 1995.

Fraser, Mary Ann. *Vicksburg: The Battle That Won the Civil War.* New York: Henry Holt, 1999.

Graymont, Barbara. *The Iroquois.* New York: Chelsea House, 1988.

Harness, Cheryl. *Mark Twain and the Queens of the Mississippi.* New York: Simon & Schuster, 1998.

Havighurst, Walter. *Upper Mississippi: A Wilderness Saga.* New York: Farrar and Rinehart, 1937.

Herb, Angela. *Beyond the Mississippi: Early Westward Expansion of the United States.* New York: Lodestar, 1996.

Holbrook, Stewart Hall. *The Columbia.* New York: Rinehart & Co., 1956.

Horgan, Paul. *Great River: The Rio Grande in North American History.* Hanover, NH: Wesleyan University Press, 1984.

Jackson, Tom. *The Ohio River.* Milwaukee: Gareth Stevens Publishing, 2004.

Ketchum, Richard, ed. *The American Heritage Book of the Revolution.* New York: American Heritage, 1958.

Longfellow, H. W. *The Song of Hiawatha.* New York: Dutton & Co., 1963.

Lourie, Peter. *Rio Grande: From the Rocky Mountains to the Gulf of Mexico.* Honesdale, PA: Boyds Mills Press, 1999.

Marrin, Albert. *Empires Lost and Won: The Spanish Heritage in the Southwest.* New York: Atheneum, 1997.

Miller, A. *The Mississippi: Life and Legends of America's Greatest River.* New York: Crescent Books, 1975.

Mylod, John. *Biography of a River: The People and Legends of the Hudson Valley.* New York: Hawthorn Books, 1969.

O'Neil, Paul. *The Rivermen.* New York: Time-Life Books, 1975.

Phelan, Mary Kay. *Waterway West: The Story of the Erie Canal.* New York: Crowell & Co., 1977.

Rawlins, Carol B. *The Colorado River.* New York: Grolier, 1999.

Reader's Digest. *Through Indian Eyes: The Untold Story of Native American Peoples.* Pleasantville, NY: 1995.

Roop, Peter, and Connie Roop, eds. *The Diary of John Wesley Powell: Conquering the Grand Canyon.* Tarrytown, NY: Marshall Cavendish, 2001.

Roop, Peter, and Connie Roop. *The Louisiana Purchase.* New York: Aladdin, 2004.

Severin, Timothy. *Explorers of the Mississippi.* New York: Knopf, 1968.

Twain, Mark. *Life on the Mississippi.* Mineola, NY: Dover, 2000.

Vestal, Stanley. *The Missouri.* Lincoln: University of Nebraska Press, 1964.

Waters, Frank. *The Colorado.* New York: Rinehart & Co., 1946.

Weil, Tom. *The Mississippi River.* New York: Hippocrene Books, Inc., 1992.

Picture Credits

© SCHOMBURG CENTER/**Art Resource, NY**: 22.

Cahokia Mounds State Historic Site: painting by William R. Iseminger: 26 (top right); Cahokia Mounds State Historic Site: 26 (bottom right).

Photograph by Jim Sturm, courtesy of **Discovery Expedition of St. Charles, MO**: 39 (left); Photograph by Edward Thomas, courtesy of Discovery Expedition of St. Charles, MO: 39 (right).

The Granger Collection, New York: 10 (right), 11, 12, 17, 18, 19, 20, 21, 27 (left), 28, 30 (right), 36, 48, 55 (right), 56, 58.

Carl E. Heilman II/Wild Visions, Inc.: 8 (left), 13.

© Marilyn Genter, **The Image Works**: 16; © Roger-Viollet/Topham/The Image Works: 23; © Frozen Images/ Rumreich/The Image Works: 24; © David R. Frazier/The Image Works: 33 (left); © Michael J. Doolittle/The Image Works: 46 (left); © Barry Sweet/The Image Works: 51; © ChromoSohm Media/The Image Works: 54; © Topham/The Image Works: 59 (right).

Independence National Historical Park: 38.

© 2007 **JupiterImages Corporation**: 4, 6, 26 (left), 34, 44, 49 (left), 52.

Wernher Krutein/Photovault.com: 14

Library of Congress, Prints and Photographs Division: LC-USZC4-994: 30 (left); Library of Congress, Prints and Photographs Division, LC-USZC2-2523: 31 (left); Library of Congress, Prints and Photographs Division, Civil War Photograph Collection, LC-USZ62-48778: 31 (middle); Library of Congress, Prints and Photographs Division, LC-USZC4-1754: 32; Library of Congress, Prints and Photographs Division, LC-USZ62-101891: 46 (right); Library of Congress, Prints and Photographs Division, LC-USZC4-8292: 50 (left); Library of Congress, Prints and Photographs Division, LC-USZ62-104700: 50 (right); Library of Congress, Prints and Photographs Division, LC-USZ62-101283: 55 (left); Library of Congress, Prints and Photographs Division, LC-USZ62-54736: 59 (left).

Courtesy of **Majestic America Line**: 33 (right).

The Mark Twain House & Museum, Hartford, CT: 31 (right).

York; Charles M. Russell; watercolor, 1908; courtesy of the **Montana Historical Society**; John Reddy photographer 10/2000: 40.

North Wind Picture Archives: 8 (right), 9, 10 (left), 27 (right), 37, 42, 43, 57.

Constance Betzer Roop: 47.

Sterling Roop: 49 (right).

Original maps on endpapers and throughout text: **Mapping Specialists, Ltd.**

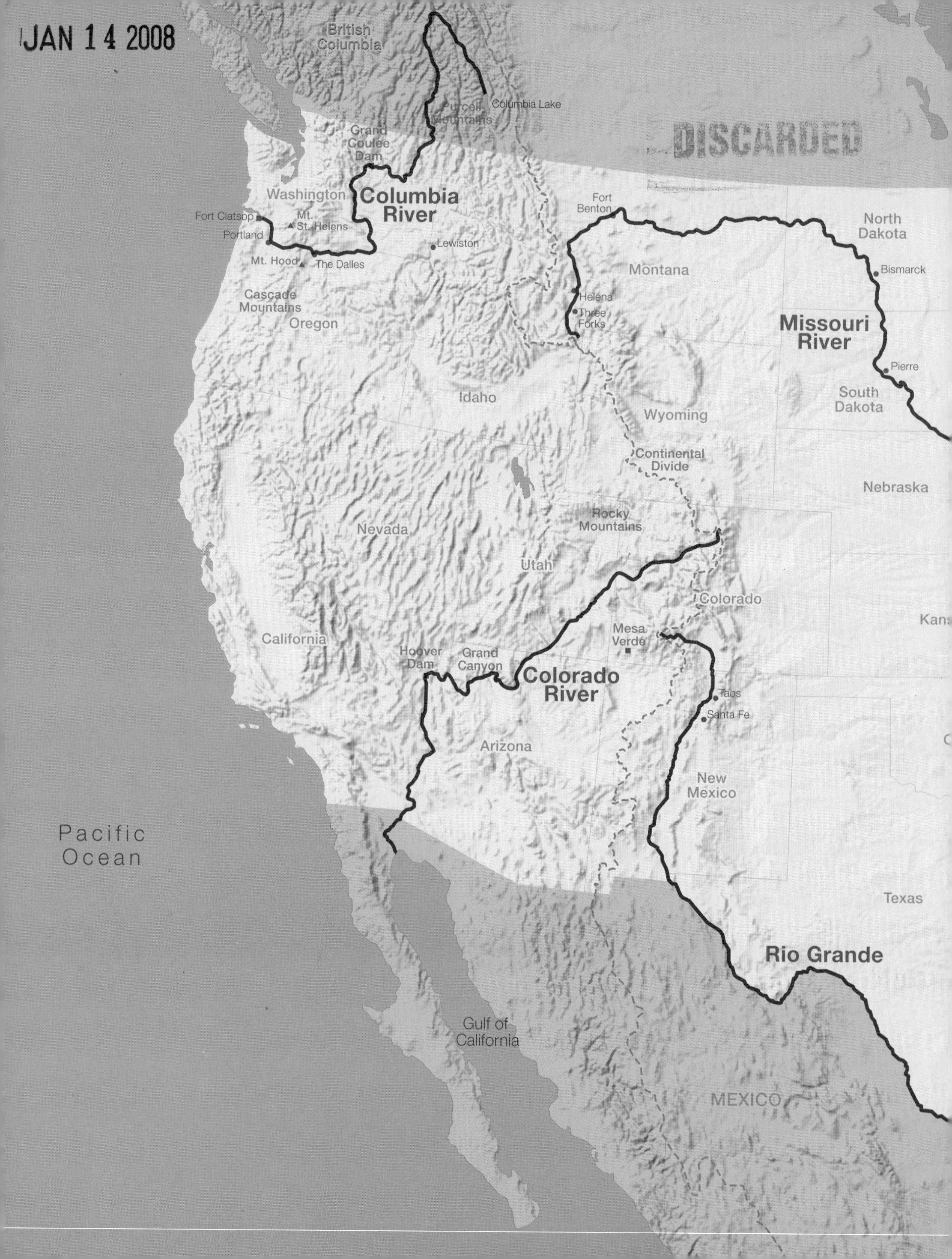
British Columbia
Purcell Mountains
Columbia Lake
Grand Coulee Dam
Washington
Columbia River
Fort Clatsop
Mt. St. Helens
Portland
Mt. Hood
The Dalles
Lewiston
Cascade Mountains
Oregon
Fort Benton
North Dakota
Bismarck
Montana
Helena
Three Forks
Missouri River
Pierre
South Dakota
Idaho
Wyoming
Continental Divide
Nebraska
Nevada
Rocky Mountains
Utah
Colorado
Kans
California
Mesa Verde
Hoover Dam
Grand Canyon
Colorado River
Taos
Santa Fe
Arizona
New Mexico
Pacific Ocean
Texas
Rio Grande
Gulf of California
MEXICO